ChatGPT Leadership Accelerator with 111 AI Prompts to Elevate Your Coaching & Mentoring Skills

ChatGPT Leadership Accelerator with 111 AI Prompts to Elevate Your Coaching & Mentoring Skills

Maximize Leadership Mastery and Peak Performance Fast and Easily with Artificial Intelligence

Mindscape Artwork Publishing
Mauricio Vasquez

Toronto, Canada

ChatGPT Leadership Accelerator with 111 AI Prompts to Elevate Your Coaching & Mentoring Skills by Mindscape Artwork Publishing [Aria Capri International Inc.]. All Rights Reserved.

All rights reserved. No part of this publication may be reproduced, distributed, shared with third parties, stored in any type of retrieval system, digitized, or transmitted in any form or by any means, including but not limited to electronic, mechanical, photocopying, recording, or otherwise, without the prior written permission of the publisher. Unauthorized reproduction or distribution of this publication, or any portion of it, may result in severe civil and criminal penalties and will be prosecuted to the fullest extent permitted by law.

Copyright © 2023, Mindscape Artwork Publishing [Aria Capri International Inc.]. All Rights Reserved.

Authors:
Mauricio Vasquez

First Printing: November 2023

ISBN-978-1-990709-87-6 (Paperback)

ISBN-978-1-998402-14-4 (Hardcover)

DEDICATION

To all devoted professionals and emerging leaders keen on career progression and leadership development: Let this book act as your go-to guide, arming you with actionable knowledge to adeptly maneuver through the intricacies of our rapidly evolving professional landscape.

INTRODUCTION

Welcome to an essential guide that seamlessly integrates time-tested methodologies in mentoring, coaching, and leadership with the avant-garde capabilities of Generative Artificial Intelligence (AI). Crafted by Mauricio Vasquez, an expert in coaching, leadership, and AI-optimized strategies, this book serves as a crucial resource for any professional committed to making a meaningful impact in today's dynamic work environment.

In the professional context characterized by rapid change, increasing complexities, and an insatiable appetite for innovation, this guide offers a set of actionable, data-backed insights, all made more accessible and applicable through the use of Generative AI. Rather than merely outlining best practices, this book is engineered to deliver tangible, measurable results that can adapt to the nuances of any professional role. The use of Generative AI is not introduced as a gimmick but as an indispensable asset. The book aims to demystify this powerful technology and demonstrate how it can be leveraged to personalize guidance, inspire innovative strategies, and create a fertile ground for transformational professional interactions.

The ultimate objective is clear-cut: to elevate your prowess in various professional capacities. Whether you're a newcomer to the professional scene, a seasoned leader in your field, or someone actively seeking avenues for innovation, this book offers practical solutions and frameworks designed to enrich your career path.

The book transcends the provision of a mere toolkit. It sets out to reshape your conceptual understanding of leadership and influence, pushing you to engage deeply with groundbreaking techniques for effective leadership and AI-prompt optimization.

Embark on this journey towards unparalleled professional excellence and influence. Prepare to redefine what it means to make a lasting, positive impact. Welcome to your next stage of professional development.

ABOUT THE AUTHOR

Mauricio Vasquez is a multifaceted professional with over 20 years of experience in risk management and insurance, specializing in sectors like mining, power, and renewable energy. He holds an Industrial Engineering degree, a Master's in Business Administration, and a Master's in Marketing and Commercial Management, along with certifications in Enterprise Risk Management and Artificial Intelligence.

Mauricio is also a certified Adler Trained Coach and a self-published author, focusing on personal growth and professional development. His expertise in Artificial Intelligence and Large Language Models Prompt engineering adds a unique layer to his professional background. Fluent in both English and Spanish, Mauricio has worked across Canada, the U.S., Latin America, and the Caribbean. In addition to his corporate roles, he is a Professional and Life Coach, committed to helping immigrants transition successfully to new lives in Canada. His approach is deeply rooted in building long-term relationships and providing tailored, impactful solutions to clients.

If you want to connect with Mauricio, go to this link
https://www.linkedin.com/in/mauriciovasquez or scan this QR code:

WHAT IS GENERATIVE ARTIFICIAL INTELLIGENCE (AI)?

In the era of Artificial Intelligence (AI), Generative AI is not just another milestone; it is an entire saga rewriting the rules of what AI can accomplish. This is not a marginal refinement in data analytics. It's artificial intelligence capable of generating text, images, or other media, using generative models.

Conventional AI excels at dissecting and interpreting existing data. Generative AI, on the other hand, elevates this by generating entirely original, value-infused content. From crafting compelling emails to architecting strategic initiatives and enhancing coaching dialogues, Generative AI amplifies human capabilities while fundamentally redefining avenues for inventive insights and solutions.

Anchored in sophisticated neural network architectures, Generative AI transcends basic mimicry to understand and extrapolate intricate human behavioral patterns. The scope of its impact is staggering, pervading diverse sectors such as marketing dynamics, C-suite leadership, and even personal self-actualization. This is not a theoretical marvel confined to the lab; it's an applied innovation with practical, immediate, and far-reaching implications.

As we pivot to the forthcoming chapter, with a focus on Natural Language Processing (NLP) Chatbots, recognize that Generative AI serves as the bedrock of these advanced conversational platforms. Within the realms of coaching, mentoring, and transformative leadership, it is Generative AI that enriches these chatbots, enabling them to produce not just relevant but deeply contextual and emotionally nuanced dialogues. The result? An elevated coaching paradigm supplemented by data-driven, yet profoundly human-like insights. To ignore the capabilities of Generative AI is to forego the boundless opportunities for innovation and enhanced efficacy it unreservedly offers.

WHAT ARE NATURAL LANGUAGE PROCESSING CHATBOTS?

An Artificial Intelligence (AI) Chatbot is a program within a website or app that uses machine learning (ML) and natural language processing (NLP) to interpret inputs and understand the intent behind a request or "prompt" (more on this later in the book). Chatbots can be rule-based with simple use cases or more advanced and able to handle multiple conversations.

The rise of language models like GPT has revolutionized the landscape of conversational AI. These Chatbots now boast advanced capabilities that can mimic not just a human conversation style but also a (super) human mind. They can find information online and produce unique content and insights.

The most important thing to know about an AI Chatbot is that it combines ML and NLP to understand what people need and bring the best answers. Some AI Chatbots are better for personal use, like conducting research, and others are best for business use, like featuring a Chatbot on your company's website.

With this in mind, we've compiled a list of the best AI Chatbots at the time of the writing of this book. We strongly suggest that you try and test each of the most popular ones and see what works best for you.

ChatGPT:
- Uses NLP to understand the context of conversations to provide related and original responses in a human-like conversation.

- Multiple use cases for things like answering questions, ideating and getting inspiration, or generating new content [like a marketing email].
- Improves over time as it has more conversations.

Microsoft Copilot/Bing Chat:
- Uses NLP and ML to understand conversation prompts.
- The compose feature can generate original written content and images, and its powerful search engine capabilities can surface answers from the web.
- It's a conversational tool, so you can continue sending messages until you're satisfied.

Google Gemini/Bard:
- Google's Bard is a multi-use AI Chatbot.
- It's powered by Google's LaMDA [instead of GPT].
- Use it for things like brainstorming and ideation, drafting unique and original content, or getting answers to your questions.
- Connected to Google's website index so it can access information from the internet.

Meta LLaMa:
- Meta's Chatbot is an open source large language [LLM].
- The tool is trained using reinforcement learning from human feedback [RLHF], learning from the preferences and ratings of human AI trainers.

Starting from now, we will refer to these platforms as Chatbots. For a guide on how to sign up to each, please refer to Appendix No 1.

If you're seeking a beginner-friendly, step-by-step guide to using ChatGPT, please refer to Appendix No. 3. This appendix includes access to our report, "Elevate Your Productivity Using ChatGPT," which offers a detailed guide on leveraging ChatGPT to boost efficiency and productivity across a range of professional environments.

As of the book's publication date, the information herein is current and accurate. The Chatbot industry, however, is dynamic, with constant updates and new entrants. While specifics may evolve, our prompts, core strategies and principles discussed in this book are designed to withstand the test of time, offering you a robust framework for navigating this fast-paced landscape.

THE BENEFITS OF USING AI CHATBOTS IN YOUR COACHING, MENTORING AND LEADERSHIP JOURNEY

Navigating the complexities of leadership, coaching, and mentorship has always been a challenging endeavor, akin to a full-time job. The introduction of Chatbots and advanced conversational agents like ChatGPT is revolutionizing this space, offering real-time, AI-generated guidance for professionals striving to excel in these domains.

These AI-driven tools are becoming invaluable assets for professional development. They offer real-time coaching, behavioral insights, and actionable strategies, which can be applied by anyone aiming to climb the corporate ladder or make an impact as a leader.

The advantages of integrating Chatbots and the insights from this book into your leadership journey can be broken down into five key areas:

1. **Time-Saving:** The promptness of Chatbots in delivering actionable advice cannot be overstated. From preparing for crucial meetings to formulating impactful leadership principles, these digital assistants can provide timely inputs that significantly shorten your learning curve.
2. **Data-Driven Quality:** Chatbots offer a reliable preliminary layer of advice and strategies, based on extensive data and algorithms. This makes them a formidable starting point for refining your own leadership or coaching plans, tailored to the complexities of your specific environment.
3. **Competitive Advantage:** In an era where tailored solutions are king, Chatbots enable you to customize your leadership or coaching approaches at an unprecedented scale. This functionality allows you to be agile and responsive, traits highly honed by effective leaders and mentors.
4. **Fresh Perspectives:** Chatbots can serve as a fertile ground for innovative ideas and practices. Leveraging AI's capability to provide data-driven suggestions, you can unearth groundbreaking approaches to leadership that might not be apparent through traditional means.
5. **Self-Empowerment:** The primary goal of this book, when coupled with Chatbots, is to enhance your sense of self-efficacy. As you interact with these technologies, you'll find tailored advice that underscores your unique strengths and challenges, thus fortifying your resolve to excel in leadership and coaching roles.

In a nutshell, combining the AI-enabled capabilities of Chatbots with the in-depth, human-centric insights in this book creates a comprehensive toolkit. This symbiosis promises to redefine and elevate traditional frameworks in leadership, coaching, and mentorship, equipping you with the resources you need to succeed in today's multifaceted professional landscape.

WHAT ARE PROMPTS?

Imagine stepping into a high-stakes negotiation with only half the information—you're likely to miss the mark. Similarly, Chatbots rely on well-crafted prompts to deliver precise and valuable responses.

Prompts serve as the guiding questions, suggestions, or ideas that instruct Chatbots on how and what to respond. But these aren't just any text or phrase; prompts are carefully engineered inputs designed to optimize the Chatbot's output for quality, relevance, and accuracy.

Prompts are suggestions, questions, or ideas for what Chatbots should respond. And for Chatbots to provide a helpful response to their users, they need a thorough prompt with some background information and relevant context. Becoming a solid prompt writer takes time and experience, but there are also some best practices that you can use to see success fairly quickly:

1. **Be precise in your instructions:** when interacting with Chatbots for leadership or coaching tasks, specificity is paramount. Clearly define the tone, scope, and objectives you wish the Chatbot to achieve. For instance, you might say, "Generate a team motivational message that emphasizes the importance of collaboration and aligns with our Q4 targets. Keep the message under 150 words and use a motivational tone."
2. **Integrate contextual information:** the more context you provide, the better Chatbots can tailor their responses. Always include any relevant background information or guidelines. For example, in the case of crafting a message to resolve team conflicts, you may want to append specific issues or arguments that the team is facing.
3. **Segment your interactions:** complex leadership tasks often have multiple components. Break these down into discrete tasks and use individual prompts for each. If you're generating materials for a leadership workshop, you could use separate prompts for the introduction, body, and conclusion segments.
4. **Continuous refinement:** Chatbots provide a valuable starting point but shouldn't replace your own expertise and voice. Use the generated material as a draft that can be further honed and personalized. This ensures that the content aligns with your unique leadership style and the specific needs of your team or mentees.
5. **Employ follow-up prompts:** to get more nuanced advice, use follow-up prompts based on initial outputs. For example, if your first prompt is, "Outline the key principles for effective leadership," a good follow-up could be, "Explain the application of each principle in remote team settings." This sequencing enriches the dialogue and makes the Chatbot's advice more actionable. Check Appendix No 2 for 1100 follow-up prompts you could use, but remember they also need to be tailored to the specific conversation you are having with the Chatbot.

HOW TO USE THIS BOOK?

In the current professional ecosystem, the topics of coaching, mentoring, and leadership are intricate but filled with unprecedented opportunities. This book offers a comprehensive guide for leveraging artificial intelligence, specifically Chatbots, to gain a competitive edge in these sectors. While the content is structured around key frameworks and principles of leadership and coaching, you are encouraged to engage with this book in a non-linear fashion, focusing on areas most relevant to your immediate and long-term objectives.

1. **Optimize your outcomes with our specialized GPT:** We are thrilled to provide exclusive access to "*My Coaching, Mentoring & Leadership Advisor*" GPT, a cutting-edge tool developed using OpenAI's ChatGPT technology. This custom GPT model is specifically designed to offer targeted assistance in leadership, coaching, and mentoring, enhancing your professional journey with AI-driven insights. To maximize its impact, we recommend using this GPT in conjunction with the prompts provided in this book. This synergistic approach will amplify your learning experience, offering a unique blend of expert guidance and personalized AI assistance. To access this GPT, please refer to the following chapter in this book.
2. **Prompt engineering for optimal outcomes:** We advocate for an informed, strategic approach to using the prompts provided in this book. Each prompt is meticulously engineered to serve a specific purpose and is accompanied by its intended goal, a guiding formula, and two illustrative examples. Text highlighted in **bold** and terms enclosed in square brackets [ ] are particularly conducive to customization. We encourage you to not just copy these prompts verbatim but to understand their underlying structure and adapt them to your unique circumstances. The more tailored the prompt, the more relevant and actionable the output will be.
3. **Differentiating complexities for broader utility:** The aim is to offer a broader perspective on how these prompts can be employed and customized. By engaging with a diverse array of prompts, you can develop a nuanced understanding of their underlying mechanisms, thereby gaining the flexibility to tailor them to multiple contexts or objectives.
4. **Integrative strategies for customization:** As you move through this book, you are encouraged to blend different strategies and tools to create customized plans. A well-crafted prompt elicits a higher-quality response; thus, investment in tailoring your inquiries is more than just a recommendation—it's a necessity for meaningful engagement with the book's content.
5. **Ethical considerations and critical thinking:** AI provides valuable insights, but it's crucial to critically evaluate this information. Use Chatbots' advice as a starting point for your strategies, complementing it with further research and ethical considerations. It's essential to remember that while AI can augment decision-making, it can't replace human wisdom.
6. **Communication excellence:** When crafting prompts for Chatbots, aim for clarity and precision. Open-ended questions often lead to more in-depth responses. For a tailored experience, you can also specify the persona or role you want the AI to assume, thereby aligning its feedback with your specific leadership or coaching context.
7. **Target audience, industry, and specificity:** Clearly defining your target audience and industry will enable you to fine-tune the strategies and insights you derive from this book and the accompanying AI resources. Whether you are a leadership consultant, executive coach, or HR professional, audience specificity enhances the utility of the guidance offered.
8. **Getting started with Chatbots:** For those new to the Chatbots platform, we provide a step-by-step guide to get you up and running, empowering you to leverage AI capabilities for your professional development in leadership and coaching.

Here is an overview of the appendices and how they can be integrated into your prompting:

- **Appendix No. 4** - Professions in Mentoring, Coaching, and Leadership: This appendix enumerates key professions that support personal and organizational development through guidance, training, and inspiration. Select the profession most relevant to your current challenge or opportunity to tailor your prompts, ensuring the most pertinent input from the Chatbot.
- **Appendix No. 5** - Specializations in Mentoring, Coaching, and Leadership: This section presents specialized roles within these fields, emphasizing excellence, innovation, and resilience in professional settings. Choose a specialization closely aligned with your specific challenge or opportunity to create effective prompts and receive the most relevant input from the Chatbot.
- **Appendix No. 6** - Tones for Responses from Chatbots: This appendix explores various writing tones you may want Chatbots to use in their responses to your prompts, ensuring alignment with your communication preferences.
- **Appendix No. 7** - Writing Styles for Responses from Chatbots: This section explores a variety of writing styles designed to enhance the clarity and effectiveness of the responses you seek to obtain from Chatbots, ensuring tailored and impactful communication.
- **Appendix No. 8** - Tagging System for Prompt Navigation: This appendix extends beyond the table of contents by offering three tags for each prompt in the book. These tags are carefully selected to assist readers in easily finding the most relevant prompts for their specific challenges or opportunities, ensuring a targeted and efficient use of the book's resources.

By strategically integrating AI tools and best practices, you can enhance not just your personal growth, but also the development of those you coach, mentor, and lead.

MEET "*MY COACHING, MENTORING & LEADERSHIP ADVISOR*" GPT

My Coaching, Mentoring & Leadership Advisor GPT, developed with OpenAI's ChatGPT technology, enhances your interaction with ChatGPT, offering a more tailored and responsive experience.

This custom GPT (Generative Pre-trained Transformer) model is expertly crafted to provide targeted help in leadership, coaching, and mentoring.

As a dynamic Artificial Intelligence companion, it aligns with your unique professional style and needs, providing tailored advice and insights to help navigate your leadership path.

Engaging with this GPT is incredibly intuitive, and simpler than you might expect. Once you access to ChatGPT, you'll be greeted by a user-friendly interface where you can input your questions or prompts.

The GPT responds almost instantly, offering valuable insights and guidance.

Whether you aim to enhance your leadership abilities, improve team dynamics, or foster personal and professional growth, *My Coaching, Mentoring & Leadership Advisor GPT* stands as your gateway to innovative professional development.

Accompanying this section there are two screenshots showcasing the user interface you'll encounter when accessing 'My Coaching, Mentoring & Leadership Advisor' GPT. This visual reference provides a clear preview of what to expect, guiding you through your first steps in utilizing this innovative tool.

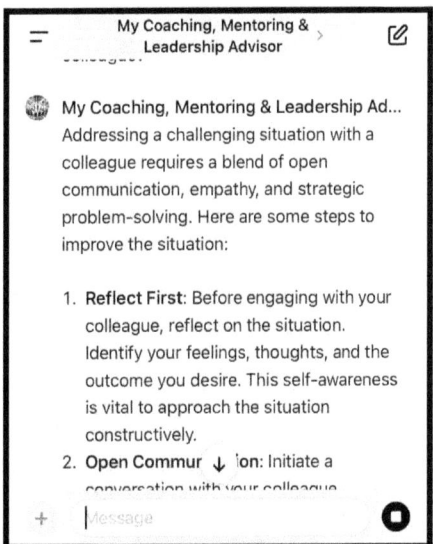

To start your journey towards advanced leadership and coaching skills, and to experience this unique blend of knowledge and technology, please scan this QR code.

Disclaimer: There's a monthly fee for using OpenAI's Plus plan, which you need to access the GPT I created for this book. Wanted to be clear – I don't get any income from OpenAI for suggesting their service. It's all about giving you great tools, and that's why I produced this GPT specifically for the book and for you. As of now, us GPT builders don't get a share of OpenAI's earnings, but if that ever changes – I'll update the disclaimer right away. Mauricio

FREE GOODWILL

Would you consider investing a minute to leave a lasting impression on someone's professional journey? Your experience and insights matter.

Right now, there's a professional, a mentor, or a leader seeking to elevate their capabilities. They're navigating the challenges of leadership, coaching, and perhaps even career transition. Your review could be a pivotal guide for them.

Think of reviews as more than just responses—they're endorsements, collective knowledge, and indicators of reliability. If this book offers you actionable insights or innovative strategies, could you share those experiences through a quick review? By doing so, you contribute to:

- Directing someone to tools and strategies that can heighten their leadership skills.
- Facilitating an individual's capacity to better mentor and coach.
- Enriching someone's perspective, which they might have otherwise overlooked.
- Catalyzing transformation in another's professional path.

By reviewing this book, you contribute to broadening the horizon of effective leadership, mentorship, and coaching for someone else. If you find value in this book, don't hesitate to share it within your network. People remember fondly those who introduced them to beneficial resources.

Enjoyed your book? Scan the QR code to quickly leave a review where you purchased it. Your feedback is invaluable!

Your engagement is much appreciated. Thank you for becoming an advocate for impactful leadership and personal development.

Best regards,

Mauricio

Scan the QR code to access our book collection.

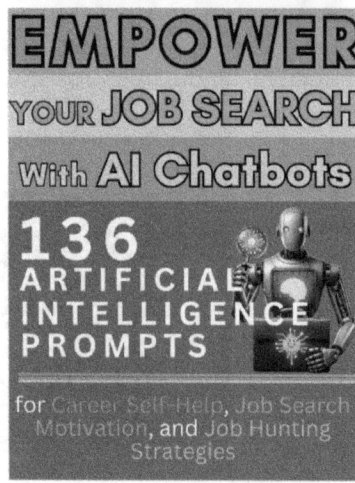

TABLE OF CONTENTS

ACCOUNTABILITY	18
ACTION	19
AWARENESS	21
BELIEF	26
CHALLENGE	29
CHANGE	32
COMMITMENT	35
CREATIVITY	36
DECISIONS	37
EXCITEMENT	38
FEAR	40
FEELINGS	42
FLOW	44
FULFILLMENT	45
GOALS	46
HABITS	49
LEARNING	51
LISTENING	57
MINDSET	59
OPTIONS	62
PERFORMANCE	65
PREFERENCES	68
PRIORITIES	69
PROGRESS	70
PURPOSE	72
RELATIONSHIPS	75
SELF-ASSESSMENT	83
SKILLS	86
STRATEGIES	88
STRENGTH	89
SUPPORT	95
VALUES	97
WEAKNESS	101

ACCOUNTABILITY

PROMPT No 1

Tags
RemoteWork - Self-Accountability - Commitment

Goal
To gain insights on methods for fostering and maintaining self-accountability within a team, enhancing their commitment to goals.

Prompt
Given the challenge of **remote work**, as a **leadership coach** and in a **supportive and encouraging tone**, could you detail methods **I** can use to maintain the **self-accountability** of my **team** towards their **goals**?

Formula
Given the challenge of [contextual challenge/opportunity], as a [profession] and in a [tone of voice], could you detail methods [I/Name/Role] can use to maintain the [desired outcome] of my [team/group/department] towards their [responsibilities/tasks/goals]?

Examples
Example 1: Given the challenge of my sales team struggling with self-motivation, as a Business Mentor and in a motivational tone, could you detail methods a new manager can use to maintain the self-accountability of their sales team towards their quarterly targets?

Example 2: Given the challenge of tight deadlines, as a Leadership Consultant and in a constructive tone, could you detail methods I can use to maintain the self-accountability of my project team towards their project deliverables?

PROMPT No 2

Tags
Strategic Plan - Team Motivation - Revenue Alignment

Goal
To obtain a comprehensive and detailed strategy that can ensure that a team remains focused on their assigned tasks and aligns with the corporate objective of increasing revenue or other objectives, including specific steps, measures, and techniques to keep the team on track and motivated to achieve this goal.

Prompt
As a **Business Consultant**, adopting a **strategic and motivational tone**, could you provide a **thorough and detailed plan** that can successfully guarantee that my team stays dedicated to their **designated tasks and works** towards the overarching corporate goal of **revenue growth**? In your response, please include **precise** steps, measures, and techniques that can be implemented to maintain the team's **focus, motivation, and alignment** with this objective.

Formula

As a **[profession]**, adopting a **[tone of voice]**, could you provide a **[detailed/thorough/comprehensive plan]** that can successfully guarantee that **[my/their]** **[team/group/department]** stays dedicated to their **[designated/assigned]** tasks and works towards the **[overarching/corporate]** goal of **[contextual challenge/opportunity]**? In your response, please include **[precise/specific]** steps, measures, and techniques that can be implemented to maintain the team's **[focus/motivation/alignment]** with this objective.

Examples

Example 1: As a Project Manager, adopting a clear and concise tone, could you provide a thorough and detailed plan that can successfully guarantee that my engineering team stays dedicated to their designated tasks and works towards the overarching goal of project completion? In your response, please include precise steps, measures, and techniques that can be implemented to maintain the team's focus, motivation, and alignment with this objective.

Example 2: As a Team Coach, adopting an encouraging and supportive tone, could you provide a comprehensive plan that can successfully guarantee that their sales team stays dedicated to their assigned tasks and works towards the corporate goal of revenue growth? In your response, please include specific steps, measures, and techniques that can be implemented to maintain the team's focus, motivation, and alignment with this objective.

ACTION

PROMPT No 3

Tags

Client Acquisition - Business Development - Detailed Strategy

Goal

To provide a comprehensive strategy for successfully attracting and acquiring new clients, thereby driving revenue growth and enhancing market position.

Prompt

Act as a **Business Development Consultant** with a specialization in **client acquisition** in the **automotive industry**. Could you provide a comprehensive and detailed response outlining **the specific steps that my team should take in order to ensure the successful attraction and acquisition of new clients**? Please include **lead generation techniques, client engagement strategies, and sales funnel optimization**. Make sure to cover **how to qualify leads and how to tailor pitches to different client needs**. Investigate unconventional **client acquisition channels** and cutting-edge **CRM technologies** to **maximize success rates**. Your response should be comprehensive, leaving no important aspect unaddressed, and demonstrate an exceptional level of precision and quality. Let's think about this step by step. Write using a **clear and concise** tone and a **tactical guide** style.

Formula

Act as a **[profession]** with a specialization in **[area of expertise]** in the **[industry]**. Could you provide a comprehensive and detailed response outlining **[specific challenge/opportunity]**? Please include **[methods/techniques]**. Make sure to cover how **[key areas/topics]**. Investigate unconventional **[area for innovation]** and cutting-edge **[technologies/methods]** to **[desired outcome]**. Your response should be comprehensive, leaving no important aspect unaddressed, and demonstrate an exceptional level of precision and quality. Let's think about this step by step. Write using a **[type]** tone and **[style]** writing style.

Examples

Example 1: Act as a Business Development Consultant with a specialization in SaaS client acquisition in the tech industry. Adopting a clear and concise tone, could you provide a comprehensive and detailed response outlining the specific steps that my team should take in order to ensure the successful attraction and acquisition of new SaaS clients? Please include inbound marketing tactics, freemium models, and customer success stories. Make sure to cover how to segment the market and how to personalize onboarding experiences. Explore the use of AI-driven analytics and chatbots for lead qualification. Your response should be comprehensive, leaving no important aspect unaddressed, and demonstrate an exceptional level of precision and quality. Let's think about this step by step. Write using a clear and concise tone and a tactical guide style.

Example 2: Act as a Business Development Consultant with a specialization in luxury goods client acquisition in the retail industry. Adopting a clear and concise tone, could you provide a comprehensive and detailed response outlining the specific steps that my team should take in order to ensure the successful attraction and acquisition of new luxury goods clients? Please include experiential marketing, exclusive events, and influencer partnerships. Make sure to cover how to identify high-net-worth individuals and how to create bespoke proposals. Delve into the use of augmented reality for product showcasing and blockchain for ensuring product authenticity. Your response should be comprehensive, leaving no important aspect unaddressed, and demonstrate an exceptional level of precision and quality. Let's think about this step by step. Write using a clear and concise tone and a tactical guide style.

PROMPT No 4

Tags
Effective Communication - Team Cooperation - Initiative Implementation
Goal
To gain insights on specific actions that can enhance communication with a team member and effectively gain their cooperation for a new initiative.
Prompt
As a **Team Leader**, adopting a **persuasive and respectful tone**, could you provide specific actions that I can take to enhance communication with a team member and effectively gain their cooperation for **a new initiative**? This is particularly relevant given the goal of **fostering effective communication and cooperation within the team**.
Formula
As a **[profession]**, adopting a **[tone of voice]**, could you provide specific actions that [I/Name/Role] can take to enhance communication with a **[team member/colleague]** and effectively gain their cooperation for a **[contextual challenge/opportunity]**? This is particularly relevant given the goal of **[desired outcome]**.
Examples

Example 1: As a Project Manager, adopting a collaborative and respectful tone, could you provide specific actions that I can take to enhance communication with a team member and effectively gain their cooperation for a new project? This is particularly relevant given the goal of fostering effective communication and cooperation within the project team.

Example 2: As a Department Head, adopting a persuasive and respectful tone, could you provide specific actions that I can take to enhance communication with a faculty member and effectively gain their cooperation for a new academic initiative? This is particularly relevant given the goal of fostering effective communication and cooperation within the faculty.

PROMPT No 5

Tags

Relationship Maintenance - Collaborative Strategies - Professional Interaction

Goal

To obtain strategies for maintaining healthy and productive relationships with colleagues or suppliers.

Prompt

Considering the importance of **maintaining healthy relationships in a professional setting**, could you, as a **leadership development consultant** and in a **collaborative tone**, share the strategies **my team** could implement to **foster such relationships** with colleagues?

Formula

Considering the importance of [contextual challenge/opportunity], could you, as a [profession] and in a [tone of voice], share the strategies [I/Name/Role]'s team could implement to [desired outcome] with [colleagues/suppliers/subordinates]?

Examples

Example 1: Considering the importance of fostering a positive work environment, could you, as a corporate trainer and in an encouraging tone, share the strategies a project team could implement to maintain healthy relationships with their colleagues?

Example 2: Could you, as a business coach and in a supportive tone, share the strategies my team could implement to maintain healthy relationships with suppliers, especially considering the importance of supplier relationship management?

AWARENESS

PROMPT No 6

Tags

False Assumptions - Insightful Leadership - Self-Reflection

Goal

To gain a detailed understanding of specific strategies and techniques that can be used to improve team members' self-awareness, particularly in recognizing and addressing potential false assumptions in their work environment.

Prompt

As a **Leadership Development Consultant**, adopting a **supportive and insightful tone**, could you provide some specific strategies and techniques that can be utilized to successfully improve the self-awareness of **my team members** when it comes to **recognizing and addressing potential false assumptions in their work environment**?

Formula

As a **[profession]**, adopting a **[tone of voice]**, could you provide some specific strategies and techniques that can be utilized to **[desired outcome]** of **[my/their]** **[team/group/department]** when it comes to **[work environment/context]**?

Examples

Example 1: As a Team Coach, adopting a supportive and insightful tone, could you provide some specific strategies and techniques that can be utilized to successfully improve the self-awareness of my project team when it comes to recognizing and addressing potential false assumptions in their project environment?

Example 2: As a Human Resources Consultant, adopting a professional and empathetic tone, could you provide some specific strategies and techniques that can be utilized to successfully improve the self-awareness of the HR department when it comes to recognizing and addressing potential false assumptions in their work environment?

PROMPT No 7

Tags

Goal-Setting - Prioritization Strategies - Task Management

Goal

To gain specific strategies or methods to effectively assist a team in identifying and establishing distinct priorities or goals, fostering an enhancement in goal-setting and prioritization within the team.

Prompt

As a **Performance Coach**, adopting a **clear and concise tone**, could you suggest specific strategies or methods that **I** can employ to effectively assist **my team** in identifying and establishing **distinct priorities or goals**? This is particularly relevant given the goal of enhancing goal-setting and prioritization within the team.

Formula

As a **[profession]**, adopting a **[tone of voice]**, could you suggest specific strategies or methods that **[I/Name/Role]** can employ to effectively assist **[my/their]** **[team/group/department]** in identifying and establishing **[contextual challenge/opportunity]**? This is particularly relevant given the goal of **[desired outcome]**.

Examples

Example 1: Adopting an encouraging and supportive tone, as a Leadership Development Consultant, could you suggest specific strategies or methods that a department head can employ to effectively assist their faculty in identifying and establishing distinct academic priorities or goals? This is particularly relevant given the goal of enhancing goal-setting and prioritization within the faculty.

Example 2: As a Talent Development Specialist, adopting an empowering and optimistic tone, could you suggest specific strategies or methods that I can employ to effectively assist my project team in identifying and establishing distinct project priorities or goals? This is particularly relevant given the goal of enhancing goal-setting and prioritization within the project team.

PROMPT No 8

Tags

Project Preparation - Team Equipping - Effective Tackling

Goal

To gain a detailed understanding of the specific actions to take to prepare a team for an upcoming project, ensuring the team is adequately equipped and ready to tackle the new project effectively.

Prompt

Given the challenge of **preparing a team for an upcoming project**, as a **Project Management Consultant** and in a **clear and concise tone**, could you provide a detailed explanation of the specific actions **I** can take to ensure that **my team** is adequately equipped and ready to **tackle the new project effectively**?

Formula

Given the challenge of **[contextual challenge/opportunity]**, as a **[profession]** and in a **[tone of voice]**, could you provide a detailed explanation of the specific actions **[I/Name/Role]** can take to ensure that **[my/their]** **[team/group/department]** is adequately equipped and ready to **[desired outcome]**?

Examples

Example 1: Given the challenge of preparing a team for an upcoming software development project, as an IT Project Manager and in a professional and solution-oriented tone, could you provide a detailed explanation of the specific actions a team leader can take to ensure that their team is adequately equipped and ready to tackle the new project effectively?

Example 2: As a Leadership Coach, in an encouraging and supportive tone, could you provide a detailed explanation of the specific actions I can take to ensure that my marketing team is adequately equipped and ready to tackle the new product launch effectively? This advice is particularly relevant given the challenge of preparing a team for an upcoming project in a competitive market.

PROMPT No 9

Tags

Effective Communication - Team Understanding - Self-Awareness Enhancement

Goal

To gain specific strategies and techniques that can be employed to ensure clear and effective communication with a team, with the ultimate goal of enhancing their self-awareness and fostering a deeper understanding among team members.

Prompt

As a **Communication Coach**, adopting a **clear and concise tone**, could you provide specific strategies and techniques that can be employed to **ensure clear and effective communication** with **my team**? This is particularly relevant given the goal of **enhancing their self-awareness and fostering a deeper understanding among team members**.

Formula

As a **[profession]**, adopting a **[tone of voice]**, could you provide specific strategies and techniques that can be employed to **[contextual challenge/opportunity]** with **[my/their]** **[team/group/department]**? This is particularly relevant given the goal of **[desired outcome]**.

Examples

Example 1: As a Team Coach, adopting a supportive and encouraging tone, could you provide specific strategies and techniques that can be employed to ensure clear and effective communication with my sales team? This is particularly relevant given the goal of enhancing their self-awareness and fostering a deeper understanding among team members.

Example 2: As a Leadership Development Consultant, adopting a professional and respectful tone, could you provide specific strategies and techniques that can be employed to ensure clear and effective communication with their research group? This is particularly relevant given the goal of enhancing their self-awareness and fostering a deeper understanding among group members.

PROMPT No 10

Tags
Alignment - Beliefs - Performance
Goal
To provide a comprehensive strategy for increasing understanding and recognition of fundamental beliefs or assumptions within teams, thereby fostering a cohesive and aligned work environment.
Prompt
Act as a **Leadership Development Consultant** with a specialization in **belief systems and team alignment** in the **aerospace industry**. Could you suggest specific actions or strategies I should implement for my team to **increase understanding and recognition of fundamental beliefs or assumptions**? Please include **cognitive mapping techniques, belief elicitation exercises, and alignment workshops**. Make sure to cover how **to identify implicit assumptions and how to align them with organizational goals**. Investigate unconventional **belief assessment tools** and cutting-edge **methods** to **enhance team cohesion**. Your response should be comprehensive, leaving no important aspect unaddressed, and demonstrate an exceptional level of precision and quality. Let's think about this step by step. Write using a **clear and concise** tone and a **strategic guide** style.
Formula
Act as a [profession] with a specialization in [area of expertise] in the [industry]. Could you suggest specific actions or strategies I should implement for my team to [specific challenge/opportunity]? Please include [methods/techniques]. Make sure to cover how [key areas/topics]. Investigate unconventional [area for innovation] and cutting-edge [technologies/methods] to [desired outcome]. Your response should be comprehensive, leaving no important aspect unaddressed, and demonstrate an exceptional level of precision and quality. Let's think about this step by step. Write using a [type] tone and [style] writing style.
Examples

Example 1: Act as a Leadership Development Consultant with a specialization in cultural alignment in the hospitality industry. Adopting a clear and concise tone, could you suggest specific actions or strategies I should implement for my customer service team to increase understanding and recognition of fundamental beliefs or assumptions? Please include value identification exercises, cross-cultural training modules, and team alignment surveys. Make sure to cover how to address cultural biases and how to integrate diverse perspectives into a unified team vision. Explore the use of AI-driven cultural assessment tools and real-time alignment dashboards. Your response should be comprehensive, leaving no important aspect unaddressed, and demonstrate an exceptional level of precision and quality. Let's think about this step by step. Write using a clear and concise tone and a strategic guide style.

Example 2: Act as a Leadership Development Consultant with a specialization in agile methodologies in the software development industry. Adopting a clear and concise tone, could you suggest specific actions or strategies I should implement for my development team to increase understanding and recognition of fundamental beliefs or assumptions? Please include agile value mapping, sprint retrospectives focused on belief alignment, and assumption audits. Make sure to cover how to identify misalignments between team practices and agile principles and how to iteratively realign them. Delve into the use of machine learning for predictive alignment and blockchain for transparent decision-making. Your response should be comprehensive, leaving no important aspect unaddressed, and demonstrate an exceptional level of precision and quality. Let's think about this step by step. Write using a clear and concise tone and a strategic guide style.

PROMPT No 11

Tags
Leadership - Action - Productivity

Goal
To gain specific actions, methods, or strategies to improve leadership abilities and successfully lead a team in creating and implementing action plans with enhanced productivity and success.

Prompt
As a **Leadership Development Consultant**, adopting a **motivational and inspiring tone**, could you provide **me** with specific actions, methods, or strategies that **I** can utilize to improve **my** leadership abilities and successfully lead **my team** in **creating and implementing action plans with enhanced productivity and success**?

Formula
As a **[profession]**, adopting a **[tone of voice]**, could you provide **[me/Name/Role]** with specific actions, methods, or strategies that **[I/Name/Role]** can utilize to improve **[my/their]** leadership abilities and successfully lead **[my/their]** **[team/group/department]** in **[contextual challenge/opportunity]**?

Examples
Example 1: As a Business Coach, adopting an encouraging and supportive tone, could you provide a department head with specific actions, methods, or strategies that they can utilize to improve their leadership abilities and successfully lead their department in creating and implementing action plans with enhanced productivity and success?

Example 2: As a Management Consultant, adopting a clear and concise tone, could you provide me with specific actions, methods, or strategies that I can utilize to improve my leadership abilities and successfully lead my project team in creating and implementing action plans with enhanced productivity and success?

BELIEF

PROMPT No 12

Tags
Verification - Evidence - Strategy

Goal
To gain a detailed understanding of the precise and comprehensive methods or techniques that can be employed to thoroughly assess and verify the evidence supporting a team's thoughts and ideas regarding their business plan or strategy.

Prompt
As a **Business Consultant**, adopting a **clear and concise tone**, could you provide me with the **precise and comprehensive methods or techniques** that can be employed to **thoroughly assess and verify the evidence supporting my team's thoughts and ideas** regarding **their business plan or strategy**?

Formula
As a **[profession]**, adopting a **[tone of voice]**, could you provide me with the **[specific methods or techniques]** that can be employed to **[desired outcome]** regarding **[contextual challenge/opportunity]**?

Examples
Example 1: As a Business Analyst, adopting a professional and analytical tone, could you provide me with the precise and comprehensive methods or techniques that can be employed to thoroughly assess and verify the evidence supporting my team's thoughts and ideas regarding their new product launch strategy?

Example 2: As a Strategic Planner, adopting a detailed and insightful tone, could you provide me with the precise and comprehensive methods or techniques that can be employed to thoroughly assess and verify the evidence supporting my team's thoughts and ideas regarding their market expansion strategy?

PROMPT No 13

Tags
Self-awareness - Improvement - Challenge

Goal
To gain a comprehensive understanding of the specific actions that can be taken to effectively challenge the team's beliefs and assumptions about themselves and their work, with the aim of fostering a culture of self-awareness and continuous improvement.

Prompt
As an **Executive Coach**, adopting a **respectful and solution-oriented tone**, could you please provide a detailed description of the specific actions that I can take to effectively challenge **my team**'s beliefs and assumptions about themselves and their work in a practical manner? This is particularly relevant given the goal of fostering a culture of self-awareness and continuous improvement.

Formula
As a **[profession]**, adopting a **[tone of voice]**, could you please provide a detailed description of the specific actions that I can take to effectively challenge **[my/their]** **[team/group/department]**'s beliefs and

assumptions about **[contextual challenge/opportunity]** in a practical manner? This is particularly relevant given the goal of **[desired outcome]**.

Examples

Example 1: As a Leadership Development Consultant, adopting a clear and concise tone, could you please provide a detailed description of the specific actions that I can take to effectively challenge my sales team's beliefs and assumptions about themselves and their work in a practical manner? This is particularly relevant given the goal of fostering a culture of self-awareness and continuous improvement.

Example 2: Adopting an encouraging and professional tone, as a Talent Management Specialist, could you please provide a detailed description of the specific actions that I can take to effectively challenge the HR department's beliefs and assumptions about themselves and their work in a practical manner? This is particularly relevant given the goal of fostering a culture of self-awareness and continuous improvement.

PROMPT No 14

Tags

Identification - Covert - Motivations

Goal

To gain insights on covertly identifying the beliefs held by team members, which can help in understanding their motivations and behavior, and in turn, guide effective team management.

Prompt

As a **Leadership Consultant**, adopting a **discreet and observant tone**, could you provide specific strategies or techniques that can be utilized to effectively and accurately discern **the beliefs held by my team**, while ensuring that **they remain unaware of my objective to gather this information**?

Formula

As a **[profession]**, adopting a **[tone of voice]**, could you provide specific strategies or techniques that can be utilized to effectively and accurately discern the **[desired outcome]**, while ensuring that **[contextual challenge/opportunity]**?

Examples

Example 1: As a Human Resources Consultant, adopting a tactful and observant tone, could you provide specific strategies or techniques that can be utilized to effectively and accurately discern the beliefs held by my sales team, while ensuring that they remain unaware of my objective to gather this information?

Example 2: As a Team Coach, adopting a discreet and understanding tone, could you provide specific strategies or techniques that can be utilized to effectively and accurately discern the beliefs held by my engineering team, while ensuring that they remain unaware of my objective to gather this information?

PROMPT No 15

Tags

Stakeholders - Interaction - Performance

Goal

To identify concrete steps that can be implemented to ensure effective communication within the team, leading to optimal performance and interaction with internal stakeholders.

Prompt

As a **Human Resources Consultant**, adopting a **solution-oriented and professional tone**, could you provide specific steps that **I** can implement to guarantee that **my HR team** excels in their communication with **internal stakeholders**, leading to **the highest level of performance possible**?

Formula

As a [profession], adopting a [tone of voice], could you provide specific steps that [I/Name/Role] can implement to guarantee that [my/their] [team/group/department] excels in their communication with [contextual challenge/opportunity], leading to [desired outcome]?

Examples

Example 1: As a Communication Specialist, adopting a clear and concise tone, could you provide specific steps that a department head can implement to guarantee that their marketing team excels in their communication with internal stakeholders, leading to the highest level of performance possible?

Example 2: As a Leadership Coach, adopting an encouraging and supportive tone, could you provide specific steps that I can implement to guarantee that my customer service team excels in their communication with internal stakeholders, leading to the highest level of performance possible?

PROMPT No 16

Tags

Viewpoints - Reevaluation - Diversity

Goal

To gain a comprehensive understanding of the specific strategies or techniques that can be employed to successfully present alternative viewpoints to the team, motivating them to reevaluate their conduct or mindset in a thoughtful manner, with the aim of fostering a culture of diverse thinking.

Prompt

As a **Leadership Development Consultant**, adopting a **respectful and solution-oriented tone**, could you please provide a detailed description of the specific strategies or techniques that I can employ to successfully present alternative viewpoints to **my team, motivating them to reevaluate their conduct or mindset in a thoughtful manner**? This is particularly relevant given the goal of fostering a culture of diverse thinking.

Formula

As a [profession], adopting a [tone of voice], could you please provide a detailed description of the specific strategies or techniques that I can employ to successfully present alternative viewpoints to [my/their] [team/group/department], [contextual challenge/opportunity]? This is particularly relevant given the goal of [desired outcome].

Examples

Example 1: As a Performance Coach, adopting a clear and concise tone, could you please provide a detailed description of the specific strategies or techniques that I can employ to successfully present alternative viewpoints to my marketing team, motivating them to reevaluate their conduct or mindset in a thoughtful manner? This is particularly relevant given the goal of fostering a culture of diverse thinking.

Example 2: Adopting an encouraging and professional tone, as a Talent Management Specialist, could you please provide a detailed description of the specific strategies or techniques that I can employ to successfully present alternative viewpoints to the HR department, motivating them to reevaluate their conduct or mindset in a thoughtful manner? This is particularly relevant given the goal of fostering a culture of diverse thinking.

PROMPT No 17

Tags

Responsibilities - Clarity - Productivity

Goal

To gain insights on the most effective strategies and approaches that can be applied during team discussions about responsibilities, with the aim of achieving maximum effectiveness, clarity, and productivity.

Prompt

As a **Team Development Specialist**, adopting a **clear and concise tone**, could you provide insights on the most effective strategies and approaches that should be considered and applied when discussing **team responsibilities**, in order to achieve the highest level of **effectiveness, clarity, and productivity**?

Formula

As a **[profession]**, adopting a **[tone of voice]**, could you provide insights on the most effective strategies and approaches that should be considered and applied when discussing **[contextual challenge/opportunity]**, in order to achieve the highest level of **[desired outcome]**?

Examples

Example 1: As a Project Manager, adopting a motivational tone, could you provide insights on the most effective strategies and approaches that should be considered and applied when discussing project responsibilities, in order to achieve the highest level of effectiveness, clarity, and productivity?

Example 2: As a Human Resources Consultant, adopting a professional tone, could you provide insights on the most effective strategies and approaches that should be considered and applied when discussing job role responsibilities, in order to achieve the highest level of effectiveness, clarity, and productivity?

CHALLENGE

PROMPT No 18

Tags

Uncertainty - Capabilities - Support

Goal

To develop strategies or approaches that can effectively assist a team in addressing any uncertainties or doubts they may have about their professional capabilities and potential within the workplace.

Prompt

As a **Leadership Coach**, adopting a **supportive and empathetic tone**, could you provide specific strategies or approaches that **I** can employ to effectively assist **my team** in addressing any **uncertainties or doubts they may have about their professional capabilities and potential** within the workplace?

Formula

As a **[profession]**, adopting a **[tone]**, could you provide specific strategies or approaches that **[I/Name/Role]** can employ to effectively assist **[my/their]** **[team/group/department]** in addressing any **[contextual challenge/opportunity]** within the workplace?

Examples

Example 1: As a Leadership Coach, adopting a supportive and empathetic tone, could you provide specific strategies or approaches that a finance department head can employ to effectively assist their accounting team in addressing any uncertainties or doubts they may have about their professional capabilities and potential within the workplace?

Example 2: As a Leadership Coach, adopting a supportive and empathetic tone, could you provide specific strategies or approaches that I can employ to effectively assist my project team in addressing any uncertainties or doubts they may have about their project management capabilities and potential within the workplace?

PROMPT No 19

Tags

Attitudes - Benefit - Mindset

Goal

To gain a detailed analysis of the specific ways in which the negative attitudes or mindset of a team might be benefiting them, fostering a deeper understanding of team dynamics and attitudes.

Prompt

As an **Emotional Intelligence Coach**, adopting an **open-minded and considerate tone**, could you provide a detailed analysis of the specific ways in which the **negative attitudes or mindset** of **my team** might be benefiting them? This is particularly relevant given the **challenge of managing pessimistic perspectives**.

Formula

As a **[profession]**, adopting a **[tone of voice]**, could you provide a detailed analysis of the specific ways in which the **[contextual challenge/opportunity]** of **[my/their]** **[team/group/department]** might be benefiting them? This is particularly relevant given the **[contextual challenge/opportunity]**

Examples

Example 1: As a Leadership Development Facilitator, adopting a patient and empathetic tone, could you provide a detailed analysis of the specific ways in which the negative attitudes or mindset of my sales team might be benefiting them? This is particularly relevant given the challenge of managing pessimistic perspectives in a high-pressure sales environment.

Example 2: Adopting a diplomatic and professional tone, as a Team Coach, could you provide a detailed analysis of the specific ways in which the negative attitudes or mindset of a project team might be benefiting them? This is particularly relevant given the challenge of managing pessimistic perspectives during a complex project.

PROMPT No 20

Tags
Motivation - Inspiration - Challenges

Goal
To gain precise and comprehensive strategies and techniques that can be used to successfully motivate and inspire team members to enthusiastically embrace new challenges and actively pursue their next major challenge.

Prompt
As a **Leadership Development Consultant**, adopting an **inspiring and motivational tone**, could you provide me with precise and comprehensive strategies and techniques that I can use to successfully **motivate and inspire my team members** to enthusiastically embrace new challenges and actively pursue their next major challenge?

Formula
As a **[profession]**, adopting a **[tone of voice]**, could you provide me with precise and comprehensive strategies and techniques that I can use to successfully **[desired outcome] [my/their] [team/group/department]** to **[contextual challenge/opportunity]**?

Examples
Example 1: As a Team Coach, adopting an encouraging and supportive tone, could you provide me with precise and comprehensive strategies and techniques that I can use to successfully motivate and inspire my sales team to enthusiastically embrace new challenges and actively pursue their next major sales target?

Example 2: As a Performance Coach, adopting an energetic and positive tone, could you provide me with precise and comprehensive strategies and techniques that I can use to successfully motivate and inspire my project team to enthusiastically embrace new project challenges and actively pursue their next major project milestone?

PROMPT No 21

Tags
Thriving - Adaptation - Insights

Goal
To gain insights on specific practices, attitudes, or behaviors that individuals can adopt to not only successfully adapt but also thrive in a new role or position.

Prompt
As a **Career Coach**, adopting a **supportive and encouraging tone**, could you share your insights on specific practices, attitudes, or behaviors that individuals can adopt **to not only successfully adapt but also thrive** in a new role or position?

Formula
As a **[profession]**, adopting a **[tone of voice]**, could you share your insights on specific practices, attitudes, or behaviors that individuals can adopt to **[contextual challenge/opportunity]** in a new role or position?

Examples

Example 1: As a Transition Coach, adopting a patient and understanding tone, could you share your insights on specific practices, attitudes, or behaviors that a newly promoted manager can adopt to not only successfully adapt but also thrive in their new leadership role? **Example 2:** As a Professional Development Consultant, adopting a motivational and positive tone, could you share your insights on specific practices, attitudes, or behaviors that a recent graduate can adopt to not only successfully adapt but also thrive in their first professional role?

PROMPT No 22

Tags

Diverse-Thinking - Problem-Solving - Leadership

Goal

To gain specific tactics or methods to encourage a team to view situations or challenges from alternative viewpoints, fostering a culture of diverse thinking and problem-solving.

Prompt

As a **Leadership Coach**, adopting an **open-minded and supportive tone**, could you suggest specific tactics or methods that **I can implement** to encourage **my team** to **view situations or challenges from alternative viewpoints**? This is particularly relevant given the goal of fostering a culture of diverse thinking.

Formula

As a [profession], adopting a [tone of voice], could you suggest specific tactics or methods that [I/Name/Role] can implement to encourage [my/their] [team/group/department] to [desired outcome]? This is particularly relevant given the [contextual challenge/opportunity].

Examples

Example 1: Adopting an encouraging and respectful tone, as a Leadership Development Consultant, could you suggest specific tactics or methods that a department head can implement to encourage their faculty to view academic challenges from alternative viewpoints? This is particularly relevant given the goal of fostering a culture of diverse thinking in an academic environment.

Example 2: As a Team Coach, adopting a collaborative and solution-oriented tone, could you suggest specific tactics or methods that I can implement to encourage my project team to view project-related challenges from alternative viewpoints? This is particularly relevant given the goal of fostering a culture of diverse thinking during complex projects.

CHANGE

PROMPT No 23

Tags

Mindset-Change - Productivity - Organizational-Development

Goal

To gain specific tactics or methods to successfully alter the mindset of a team, fostering a change in mindset for enhanced productivity and overall effectiveness.

Prompt

As an **Organizational Development (OD) Consultant**, adopting an **encouraging and solution-oriented tone**, could you suggest specific tactics or methods that **I** can employ to **successfully alter the mindset** of **my team**? This is particularly relevant given the ultimate goal of **enhancing their productivity and overall effectiveness**.

Formula

As a [profession], adopting a [tone of voice], could you suggest specific tactics or methods that [I/Name/Role] can employ to [desired outcome] of [my/their] [team/group/department]? This is particularly relevant given the ultimate goal of [desired outcome].

Examples

Example 1: Adopting a motivational and enthusiastic tone, as a Leadership Development Facilitator, could you suggest specific tactics or methods that a department head can employ to successfully alter the mindset of their faculty? This is particularly relevant given the ultimate goal of enhancing their academic productivity and overall effectiveness.

Example 2: As a Performance Coach, adopting an empowering and optimistic tone, could you suggest specific tactics or methods that I can employ to successfully alter the mindset of my sales team? This is particularly relevant given the ultimate goal of enhancing their sales productivity and overall effectiveness.

PROMPT No 24

Tags

Celebration - Team-Morale - Appreciation

Goal

To gain specific details and suggestions on how to make the celebration of a successful work or project more memorable and meaningful for everyone involved, fostering team morale and appreciation.

Prompt

As a **Team Building Specialist**, adopting an **enthusiastic and appreciative tone**, could you provide specific details and suggestions on how **I** can improve and make the celebration of a successful **work or project** that **my team** has accomplished more memorable and meaningful for everyone involved? This is particularly relevant given the goal of **fostering team morale and appreciation**.

Formula

As a [profession], adopting a [tone of voice], could you provide specific details and suggestions on how [I/Name/Role] can improve and make the celebration of a successful [work/project/task] that [my/their] [team/group/department] has accomplished more memorable and meaningful for everyone involved? This is particularly relevant given the goal of [desired outcome].

Examples

Example 1: As a Corporate Event Planner, adopting an enthusiastic and appreciative tone, could you provide specific details and suggestions on how a department head can improve and make the celebration of a successful project that their IT team has accomplished more memorable and meaningful for everyone involved? This is particularly relevant given the goal of fostering team morale and appreciation within the IT department.

Example 2: As a Motivational Speaker, adopting an energetic and appreciative tone, could you provide specific details and suggestions on how I can improve and make the celebration of a successful work that my sales team has accomplished more memorable and meaningful for everyone involved? This is particularly relevant given the goal of fostering team morale and appreciation within the sales team.

PROMPT No 25

Tags
Proposal-Development - Positive-Change - Work-Habits

Goal
To create a thorough and successful proposal for a team, with the aim of transforming their work routine and overall attitude, fostering a positive change in work habits and mindset.

Prompt
As a **Leadership Development Consultant**, adopting an **empowering and optimistic tone**, could you guide **me** through the specific steps **I** can take to create a thorough and successful proposal for **my team**? The goal is to successfully **transform their work routine and overall attitude**, fostering **a positive change in work habits and mindset**.

Formula
As a [profession], adopting a [tone of voice], could you guide [me/Name/Role] through the specific steps [I/Name/Role] can take to create a thorough and successful proposal for [my/their] [team/group/department]? The goal is to successfully [desired outcome], fostering [contextual challenge/opportunity].

Examples
Example 1: Adopting an encouraging and professional tone, as a Team Coach, could you guide a department head through the specific steps they can take to create a thorough and successful proposal for their faculty? The goal is to successfully transform their teaching routine and overall attitude, fostering a positive change in teaching habits and mindset. **Example 2:** As a Change Management Consultant, adopting a clear and concise tone, could you guide me through the specific steps I can take to create a thorough and successful proposal for my project team? The goal is to successfully transform their project management routine and overall attitude, fostering a positive change in project management habits and mindset.

PROMPT No 26

Tags
Assessment - Improvement - Team-Development

Goal
To gain a clear understanding of the specific factors or criteria that should be considered when assessing areas that need improvement within a team, fostering effective team development and performance enhancement.

Prompt
As a **Performance Improvement Consultant**, adopting a **clear and concise tone**, could you elaborate on the specific factors or criteria that **I** should consider when assessing **areas that need improvement** within **my**

team? This is particularly relevant given the goal of **fostering effective team development and performance enhancement**.

Formula

As a **[profession]**, adopting a **[tone of voice]**, could you elaborate on the specific factors or criteria that **[I/Name/Role]** should consider when assessing **[contextual challenge/opportunity]** within **[my/their]** **[team/group/department]**? This is particularly relevant given the goal of **[desired outcome]**.

Examples

Example 1: As a Team Development Specialist, adopting a respectful and professional tone, could you elaborate on the specific factors or criteria that a department head should consider when assessing areas that need improvement within their faculty? This is particularly relevant given the goal of fostering effective academic development and performance enhancement.

Example 2: As an Organizational Development Consultant, adopting a supportive and diplomatic tone, could you elaborate on the specific factors or criteria that I should consider when assessing areas that need improvement within my project team? This is particularly relevant given the goal of fostering effective project development and performance enhancement.

COMMITMENT

PROMPT No 27

Tags

Communication - Promotion - Motivation

Goal

To learn effective methods to subtly communicate to a team about the potential for a promotion or salary increase, contingent on performance improvement, fostering motivation and performance enhancement.

Prompt

As a **Human Resources Consultant**, adopting a **diplomatic and professional tone**, could you suggest specific and effective methods that **I** can use to subtly convey to **my team** that they have the potential for a **promotion or salary increase**, without directly stating it, as long as **they improve their performance**? This is particularly relevant given the goal of fostering motivation and performance enhancement.

Formula

As a **[profession]**, adopting a **[tone of voice]**, could you suggest specific and effective methods that **[I/Name/Role]** can use to subtly convey to **[my/their]** **[team/group/department]** that they have the potential for **[contextual challenge/opportunity]**, without directly stating it, as long as they **[contextual challenge/opportunity]**? This is particularly relevant given the goal of **[desired outcome]**

Examples

Example 1: As a Corporate Trainer, adopting a diplomatic and professional tone, could you suggest specific and effective methods that a department head can use to subtly convey to their faculty that they have the potential for a promotion or salary increase, without directly stating it, as long as they improve their academic performance? This is particularly relevant given the goal of fostering motivation and performance enhancement among the faculty.

Example 2: As a Leadership Coach, adopting a diplomatic and professional tone, could you suggest specific and effective methods that I can use to subtly convey to my project team that they have the potential for a promotion or salary increase, without directly stating it, as long as they improve their project performance? This is particularly relevant given the goal of fostering motivation and performance enhancement within the project team.

CREATIVITY

PROMPT No 28

Tags
Satisfaction - Engagement - Productivity
Goal
To gain insights on ways to enhance job satisfaction and enjoyment in a team, thereby improving their engagement and productivity.
Prompt
Considering the importance of **job satisfaction in team productivity**, as an **employee engagement manager** and in an **optimistic and enthusiastic tone**, could you propose ways **my team** can find more enjoyment in accomplishing their **responsibilities**?
Formula
Considering the importance of [contextual challenge/opportunity], as a [profession] and in a [tone of voice], could you propose ways [I/Name/Role]'s [team/group/department] can find more enjoyment in accomplishing their [responsibilities/tasks/goals]?
Examples
Example 1: Considering the importance of job satisfaction in a customer service team, as a human resources manager and in a supportive and friendly tone, could you propose ways a team leader can help their team find more enjoyment in accomplishing their customer service responsibilities? **Example 2:** As a corporate trainer, in an inspiring and motivating tone, could you propose ways I can help my sales team find more enjoyment in accomplishing their sales targets, particularly considering the importance of job satisfaction in sales performance?

PROMPT No 29

Tags
Responsibility - Service - Contribution
Goal
To gain comprehensive explanations and specific examples of effective strategies to enhance and broaden a team's responsibilities and influence in serving others, maximizing the team's overall contribution in serving others.
Prompt

As a **Leadership Development Consultant**, adopting an **encouraging and supportive tone**, could you provide comprehensive explanations and specific examples of effective strategies that **my team** can implement to enhance and broaden **their** responsibilities and influence in serving others? This is particularly relevant given the goal of **maximizing our team's overall contribution in serving others**.

Formula

As a [profession], adopting a [tone of voice], could you provide comprehensive explanations and specific examples of effective strategies that [I/Name/Role] can implement to enhance and broaden [my/their] [team/group/department]'s responsibilities and influence in serving others? This is particularly relevant given the goal of [desired outcome].

Examples

Example 1: Adopting an optimistic and enthusiastic tone, as a Team Coach, could you provide comprehensive explanations and specific examples of effective strategies that a department head can implement to enhance and broaden their faculty's responsibilities and influence in serving others? This is particularly relevant given the goal of maximizing the faculty's overall contribution in serving others.

Example 2: As a Leadership Trainer, adopting a respectful and collaborative tone, could you provide comprehensive explanations and specific examples of effective strategies that I can implement to enhance and broaden my project team's responsibilities and influence in serving others? This is particularly relevant given the goal of maximizing our project team's overall contribution in serving others.

DECISIONS

PROMPT No 30

Tags

Timelines - Realism - Performance

Goal

To gain insights on the basis or criteria a team should consider when setting realistic timelines for their performance goals or tasks.

Prompt

Considering the challenge of **setting realistic timelines for performance goals or tasks**, as a **Performance Management Specialist** and in a **clear and concise tone**, could you come up with the basis **my team** could consider for **this purpose**?

Formula

Considering the challenge of [contextual challenge/opportunity], as a [profession] and in a [tone of voice], could you come up with the basis [I/Name/Role]'s [team/group/department] could consider for [desired outcome]?

Examples

Example 1: Considering the challenge of setting realistic timelines for project deliverables, as a Project Management Consultant and in a solution-oriented tone, could you come up with the basis a project team could consider for this purpose?

Example 2: As a Time Management Specialist, in a professional and supportive tone, could you come up with a basis my sales team could consider to produce a realistic time frame for them to accomplish their sales targets, especially considering the challenge of managing multiple accounts?

PROMPT No 31

Tags
Ethics - Decision-Making - Alignment

Goal
To gain specific strategies, methods, and examples on how to effectively integrate ethical considerations into the business decision-making process, ensuring that actions align with the company's ethical standards and values.

Prompt
As a **Business Ethics Consultant**, adopting a **professional and respectful tone**, could you provide a comprehensive response that includes specific strategies, methods, and examples on how **we** can effectively integrate **ethical considerations into our business decision-making process?** This is particularly relevant given the goal of **ensuring that our actions align with our ethical standards and values**.

Formula
As a **[profession]**, adopting a **[tone of voice]**, could you provide a comprehensive response that includes specific strategies, methods, and examples on how **[I/Name/Role]** can effectively integrate **[contextual challenge/opportunity]**? This is particularly relevant given the goal of **[desired outcome]**.

Examples
Example 1: As a Corporate Social Responsibility Advisor, adopting a clear and concise tone, could you provide a comprehensive response that includes specific strategies, methods, and examples on how a department head can effectively integrate ethical considerations into their department's decision-making process? This is particularly relevant given the goal of ensuring that their actions align with the department's ethical standards and values.

Example 2: As an Organizational Development Consultant, adopting a professional and understanding tone, could you provide a comprehensive response that includes specific strategies, methods, and examples on how I can effectively integrate ethical considerations into my team's business decision-making process? This is particularly relevant given the goal of ensuring that our actions align with our team's ethical standards and values.

EXCITEMENT

PROMPT No 32

Tags
Professional-Development - C-suite - Effectiveness

Goal

To gain specific methods, techniques, and practices that can be utilized to guarantee the utmost effectiveness and comprehensiveness of professional development programs for C-suite executives, with the aim of enhancing their skills, knowledge, and overall performance to the greatest extent possible.

Prompt

As a **Leadership Development Consultant**, adopting a **professional and insightful tone**, could you provide specific methods, techniques, and practices that **I** can utilize to guarantee the utmost effectiveness and comprehensiveness of professional development programs for **C-suite executives**? The goal is to **enhance their skills, knowledge, and overall performance to the greatest extent possible**.

Formula

As a [profession], adopting a [tone of voice], could you provide specific methods, techniques, and practices that [I/Name/Role] can utilize to guarantee the utmost effectiveness and comprehensiveness of professional development programs for [contextual challenge/opportunity]? The goal is to [desired outcome].

Examples

Example 1: As a Corporate Trainer, adopting a knowledgeable and engaging tone, could you provide specific methods, techniques, and practices that a Human Resources Manager can utilize to guarantee the utmost effectiveness and comprehensiveness of professional development programs for their C-suite executives? The goal is to enhance their skills, knowledge, and overall performance to the greatest extent possible.

Example 2: As an Executive Coach, adopting a professional and supportive tone, could you provide specific methods, techniques, and practices that a supply chain manager can utilize to guarantee the utmost effectiveness and comprehensiveness of professional development programs for their supply chain team? The goal is to enhance their skills, knowledge, and overall performance to the greatest extent possible.

PROMPT No 33

Tags

Rejuvenation - Support - Energy

Goal

To gain specific strategies or actions that can be implemented to effectively support and uplift a team when a significant decline in their energy levels is observed, fostering a rejuvenated and energetic work environment.

Prompt

As a **Leadership Development Consultant**, adopting an **encouraging and supportive tone**, could you suggest specific strategies or actions that **I** can implement to effectively support and uplift **my team** when I observe a significant decline in their energy levels? This is particularly relevant given the goal of **fostering a rejuvenated and energetic work environment**.

Formula

As a [profession], adopting a [tone of voice], could you suggest specific strategies or actions that [I/Name/Role] can implement to effectively support and uplift [my/their] [team/group/department] when [I/Name/Role] observe a significant decline in their energy levels? This is particularly relevant given the goal of [desired outcome].

Examples

Example 1: As a Team Coach, adopting a motivating and positive tone, could you suggest specific strategies or actions that a financial reporting manager can implement to effectively support and uplift their finance team when they observe a significant decline in their energy levels? This is particularly relevant given the goal of fostering a rejuvenated and energetic finance environment.

Example 2: As an Executive Coach, adopting an inspiring and supportive tone, could you suggest specific strategies or actions that I can implement to effectively support and uplift my sales team when I observe a significant decline in their energy levels? This is particularly relevant given the goal of fostering a rejuvenated and energetic sales environment.

PROMPT No 34

Tags

Conflict-Resolution - Relationship - Positivity

Goal

To gain specific strategies and approaches that can be implemented to effectively handle conflicts among team members, ensuring that not only are the issues resolved, but also that the overall working relationship is enhanced and becomes more positive and satisfying.

Prompt

As a **Conflict Resolution Specialist**, adopting a **diplomatic and solution-oriented tone**, could you provide specific strategies and approaches that **I** can implement to effectively handle conflicts among **my team members**, ensuring that not only are the issues resolved, but also that the overall working relationship is **enhanced and becomes more positive and satisfying**?

Formula

As a **[profession]**, adopting a **[tone of voice]**, could you provide specific strategies and approaches that **[I/Name/Role]** can implement to effectively handle conflicts among **[my/their]** **[team/group/department]**, ensuring that not only are the issues resolved, but also that the overall working relationship is **[desired outcome]**?

Examples

Example 1: As a Team Coach, adopting a respectful and patient tone, could you provide specific strategies that a customer service head can implement to effectively handle conflicts among their team, ensuring that not only are the issues resolved, but also that the overall working relationship is enhanced and becomes more positive and satisfying?

Example 2: As a Leadership Development Consultant, adopting a professional and understanding tone, could you provide specific approaches that I can implement to effectively handle conflicts among my supply chain team, ensuring that not only are the issues resolved, but also that the overall working relationship is enhanced and becomes more positive and satisfying?

FEAR

PROMPT No 35

Tags

Empathy - Anxiety - Workplace

Goal

To gain specific strategies and actions that leaders can implement to establish a nurturing and empathetic workplace atmosphere that effectively assists employees in managing and overcoming feelings of fear or anxiety while on the job.

Prompt

As a **Leadership Development Consultant**, adopting a **compassionate and understanding tone**, could you provide specific strategies and actions that **I**, as a leader, can implement to establish a **nurturing and empathetic workplace atmosphere** that effectively assists **my employees** in managing and overcoming feelings of fear or anxiety while on the job?

Formula

As a [profession], adopting a [tone of voice], could you provide specific strategies and actions that [I/Name/Role], as a leader, can implement to establish a [desired outcome] that effectively assists [my/their] [team/group/department] in managing and overcoming feelings of fear or anxiety while on the job?

Examples

Example 1: As a Human Resources Consultant, adopting a supportive and empathetic tone, could you provide specific strategies and actions that a manufacturing department head can implement to establish a nurturing and empathetic workplace atmosphere that effectively assists their manufacturing team in managing and overcoming feelings of fear or anxiety while on the job?

Example 2: As a Business Coach, adopting a patient and understanding tone, could you provide specific strategies and actions that I, as a office management leader, can implement to establish a nurturing and empathetic workplace atmosphere that effectively assists my team in managing and overcoming feelings of fear or anxiety while on the job?

PROMPT No 36

Tags

Resilience - Inspiration - Support

Goal

To gain insights on how a leader can effectively demonstrate confidence and resilience to inspire and support team members in overcoming fear and discouragement, fostering a resilient and confident team.

Prompt

As a **Leadership Coach**, adopting an **inspiring and supportive tone**, could you provide insights on how **I**, as a leader, can effectively **demonstrate confidence and resilience** to inspire and support **my team members** in **overcoming fear and discouragement**? This is particularly relevant given the goal of **fostering a resilient and confident team**.

Formula

As a [profession], adopting a [tone of voice], could you provide insights on how [I/Name/Role], as a leader, can effectively [desired outcome] to inspire and support [my/their] [team/group/department] in [contextual challenge/opportunity]? This is particularly relevant given the goal of [desired outcome].

Examples

Example 1: As a Team Development Specialist, adopting a motivational and empathetic tone, could you provide insights on how an event planning department head can effectively demonstrate confidence and resilience to inspire and support their team in overcoming fear and discouragement? This is particularly relevant given the goal of fostering a resilient and confident event planning event.

Example 2: As a Performance Coach, adopting an encouraging and positive tone, could you provide insights on how I, as a construction project manager, can effectively demonstrate confidence and resilience to inspire and support my construction team in overcoming fear and discouragement? This is particularly relevant given the goal of fostering a resilient and confident team.

FEELINGS

PROMPT No 37

Tags
Emotional-Intelligence - Leadership - Responsiveness

Goal
To gain insights on the most effective strategies and techniques for integrating emotional intelligence principles into leadership and management approaches, enhancing comprehension and responsiveness towards emotions within the workplace.

Prompt
As an **Emotional Intelligence Coach**, adopting a **supportive and understanding tone**, could you provide insights on the most effective strategies and techniques for integrating **emotional intelligence principles** into **my leadership and management approaches**? How can these principles be utilized to **enhance comprehension and responsiveness towards emotions within the workplace**?

Formula
As a [profession], adopting a [tone of voice], could you provide insights on the most effective strategies and techniques for integrating [contextual challenge/opportunity] into [I/Name/Role]'s [team/group/department]'s [contextual challenge/opportunity]? How can these principles be utilized to [desired outcome]?

Examples
Example 1: As a Leadership Development Consultant, adopting a professional and empathetic tone, could you provide insights on the most effective strategies and techniques for integrating emotional intelligence principles into a department head's faculty management approaches? How can these principles be utilized to enhance comprehension and responsiveness towards emotions within the faculty?

Example 2: As a Performance Coach, adopting a respectful and understanding tone, could you provide insights on the most effective strategies and techniques for integrating emotional intelligence principles into my technical support management approaches? How can these principles be utilized to enhance comprehension and responsiveness towards emotions within the technical support team?

PROMPT No 38

Tags
Dissatisfaction - Morale - Promotion

Goal

To gain specific steps or techniques that can be implemented to successfully manage and provide assistance to a team member who is experiencing emotional distress or dissatisfaction as a result of being passed over for a promotion or salary increase.

Prompt

As a **Human Resources Consultant**, adopting a **compassionate and understanding tone**, could you provide specific steps or techniques that can be implemented to successfully manage and provide assistance to **a team member** who is experiencing **emotional distress or dissatisfaction as a result of being passed over for a promotion or salary increase**? This is particularly relevant given the goal of **maintaining morale and productivity in the face of career disappointments**.

Formula

As a [profession], adopting a [tone of voice], could you provide specific steps or techniques that can be implemented to successfully manage and provide assistance to a [team member/colleague] who is experiencing [contextual challenge/opportunity]? This is particularly relevant given the goal of [desired outcome].

Examples

Example 1: As a Leadership Coach, adopting a supportive and empathetic tone, could you provide specific steps or techniques that can be implemented to successfully manage and provide assistance to a team member who is experiencing emotional distress or dissatisfaction as a result of not achieving their expected performance targets? This is particularly relevant given the goal of maintaining morale and productivity in the face of performance-related disappointments.

Example 2: As a Career Counselor, adopting a patient and understanding tone, could you provide specific steps or techniques that can be implemented to successfully manage and provide assistance to a client who is experiencing emotional distress or dissatisfaction as a result of not securing their desired job? This is particularly relevant given the goal of maintaining optimism and resilience in the face of job search disappointments.

PROMPT No 39

Tags

Roles - Emotional-Intelligence - Cohesion

Goal

To gain detailed insights on ways to assist a team in exploring and discussing the impact of roles, team dynamics, and other factors on their emotional states, enhancing emotional intelligence and team cohesion.

Prompt

Given the importance of **understanding the impact of roles and team dynamics on emotional states**, as an **Emotional Intelligence Coach** and in an **empathetic and patient tone**, could you explain in detail the ways in which I can assist **my team** in exploring and discussing **these factors**?

Formula

Given the importance of [contextual challenge/opportunity], as a [profession] and in a [tone of voice], could you explain in detail the ways in which [I/Name/Role] can assist [my/their] [team/group/department] in exploring and discussing [specific factors]?

Examples

Example 1: Given the importance of understanding the impact of personal problems on the emotional state of a colleague, as a Team Coach and in a supportive and understanding tone, could you explain in detail the ways in which a project manager can assist their colleague in exploring and discussing these factors?

Example 2: As a Leadership Development Facilitator, in a respectful and open-minded tone, could you explain in detail the ways in which I can assist my finance team in exploring and discussing the impact of their individual roles, team dynamics, or any other relevant factors on their emotional states and overall mood, especially considering the importance of emotional intelligence in financial performance?

FLOW

PROMPT No 40

Tags

Metrics - Productivity - Influence

Goal

To understand specific methods or metrics that can be used to accurately assess the influence of 'flow' on both the productivity and success of a team and the overall outcomes of a business.

Prompt

As a **Business Performance Consultant**, adopting an **analytical and insightful tone**, could you suggest specific methods or metrics that **I** can use to accurately assess the influence of **'flow'** on both the **productivity and success** of **my team** and the overall outcomes of our business?

Formula

As a [profession], adopting a [tone of voice], could you suggest specific methods or metrics that [I/Name/Role] can use to accurately assess the influence of [contextual challenge/opportunity] on both the [desired outcome] of [my/their] [team/group/department] and the overall outcomes of our business?

Examples

Example 1: As a Team Performance Coach, adopting a data-driven and insightful tone, could you suggest specific methods or metrics that an engineering team manager can use to accurately assess the influence of 'flow' on both the productivity and success of their engineering team and the overall outcomes of their work?

Example 2: As a Leadership Development Consultant, adopting an analytical and strategic tone, could you suggest specific methods or metrics that I can use to accurately assess the influence of 'flow' on both the productivity and success of my internal audit team and the overall outcomes of their review targets?

PROMPT No 41

Tags

Diversity - Engagement - Fulfillment

Goal

To understand how to utilize the unique and diverse experiences of team members, particularly their levels of engagement and fulfillment, in order to design and implement strategies that will create a highly motivating and satisfying work environment for everyone involved.

Prompt

As a **Leadership Development Consultant**, adopting a **supportive and encouraging tone**, could you provide specific ways in which I can utilize the unique and diverse experiences of my **team members**, particularly their **levels of engagement and fulfillment**, to effectively design and implement strategies that will result in **a highly motivating and satisfying work environment for everyone involved**?

Formula

As a [profession], adopting a [tone of voice], could you provide specific ways in which [I/Name/Role] can utilize the unique and diverse experiences of my [team/group/department], particularly their [contextual challenge/opportunity], to effectively design and implement strategies that will result in a [desired outcome]?

Examples

Example 1: As a Team Coach, adopting a motivational and positive tone, could you provide specific ways in which a business intelligence team manager can utilize the unique and diverse experiences of their business intelligence team, particularly their levels of engagement and fulfillment, to effectively design and implement strategies that will result in a highly motivating and satisfying work environment for everyone involved?

Example 2: As an Executive Coach, adopting an inspiring and supportive tone, could you provide specific ways in which I can utilize the unique and diverse experiences of my technical support team, particularly their levels of engagement and fulfillment, to effectively design and implement strategies that will result in a highly motivating and satisfying work environment for everyone involved?

FULFILLMENT

PROMPT No 42

Tags

Attributes - Leadership - Empathy

Goal

To gain insights on the specific personal attributes, abilities, or shifts in mindset that one should prioritize cultivating within themselves to become an exceptionally effective leader, especially considering a current deficiency in abilities.

Prompt

As a **Leadership Development Consultant**, adopting a **supportive and constructive tone**, could you guide **me** on the precise personal attributes, abilities, or shifts in mindset **I** should prioritize cultivating within **myself** to become an exceptionally effective **leader**? This is particularly relevant given my current deficiency in empathy towards my team members.

Formula

As a [profession], adopting a [tone of voice], could you guide [me/Name/Role] on the precise personal attributes, abilities, or shifts in mindset [I/Name/Role] should prioritize cultivating within [myself/themselves] to become an exceptionally effective [leader/role]? This is particularly relevant given [contextual challenge/opportunity].

Examples

Example 1: As a Leadership Coach, adopting a compassionate and encouraging tone, could you guide a department head on the precise personal attributes, abilities, or shifts in mindset they should prioritize cultivating within themselves to become an exceptionally effective leader? This is particularly relevant given their current deficiency in empathy towards their faculty.

Example 2: As a Personal Development Coach, adopting a motivational and positive tone, could you guide me on the precise personal attributes, abilities, or shifts in mindset I should prioritize cultivating within myself to become an exceptionally effective project manager? This is particularly relevant given my current deficiency in empathy towards my project team.

GOALS

PROMPT No 43

Tags

Evaluation - Growth - KPIs

Goal

To gain insights on how to effectively measure and evaluate the professional growth of a team in a specific skill, including the implementation of specific key performance indicators (KPIs) and the use of methods or tools for monitoring and assessing the progress of the development process.

Prompt

As a **Human Resources Consultant**, adopting a **clear and concise tone**, could you provide insights on how **I** can effectively measure and evaluate the professional growth of **my team** in in their **problem solving skills**? Please provide specific key performance indicators (KPIs) that can be implemented for this purpose. Furthermore, what methods or tools can be utilized to accurately monitor and assess the progress of this development process?

Formula

As a [profession], adopting a [tone of voice], could you provide insights on how [I/Name/Role] can effectively measure and evaluate the professional growth of [my/their] [team/group/department] in [contextual challenge/opportunity]? Please provide specific key performance indicators (KPIs) that can be implemented for this purpose. Furthermore, what methods or tools can be utilized to accurately monitor and assess the progress of this development process?

Examples

Example 1: As a Performance Management Consultant, adopting a detailed and analytical tone, could you provide insights on how a department head can effectively measure and evaluate the professional growth of their faculty in their critical thinking skills? Please provide specific key performance indicators (KPIs) that can be implemented for this purpose. Furthermore, what methods or tools can be utilized to accurately monitor and assess the progress of this development process?

Example 2: As a Leadership Development Consultant, adopting a supportive and encouraging tone, could you provide insights on how I can effectively measure and evaluate the professional growth of my project team in their communication skills? Please provide specific key performance indicators (KPIs) that can be implemented for this purpose. Furthermore, what methods or tools can be utilized to accurately monitor and assess the progress of this development process?

PROMPT No 44

Tags
Collaboration - Frameworks - Cohesiveness

Goal
To explore various frameworks, methodologies, or strategies that can be employed by a team to align their efforts, increase collaboration, and effectively work towards achieving their collective goals.

Prompt
Act as a **Team Development Specialist** specializing in the **corporate training industry**. Could you provide an **exhaustive overview of the different frameworks, methodologies, or strategies that my team and I could consider implementing to work cohesively and effectively toward our goals**? This includes **strategies that are both well-established and those that might be unconventional but effective**. Provide unique insights and overlooked opportunities, considering various team dynamics, organizational structures, and industries. Let's analyze this piece by piece. Write using an informative tone and analytical writing style.

Formula
Act as a [profession] specializing in the [industry]. Could you provide [contextual challenge/opportunity]? This includes [desired outcome]. Provide unique insights and overlooked opportunities, considering various team dynamics, organizational structures, and industries. Let's analyze this piece by piece. Write using a [type] tone and [style] writing style.

Examples
Example 1: Act as a Leadership Coach specializing in the healthcare industry. Could you provide a meticulous and wide-ranging response on the frameworks that a medical team could adopt to improve collaboration and work towards shared goals? Include uncommon advice and underrated resources. Let's dissect this carefully. Write using an instructive tone and engaging writing style.

Example 2: Act as a Performance Coach specializing in the technology industry. Could you provide a comprehensive and elaborate depiction of the strategies that a tech team could consider implementing to enhance performance and align with organizational goals? Share distinctive guidance and unexplored options. Let's think about this step by step. Write using a confident tone and constructive writing style.

PROMPT No 45

Tags
Assessment - Performance - Accountability

Goal
to assist you in evaluating the current progress of your team members towards achieving set goals. It aims to provide a comprehensive framework for tracking, measuring, and assessing performance, identifying gaps or areas of improvement, and implementing strategies to ensure alignment with the desired outcomes.

Prompt
Act as a **Performance Management Expert** specializing in the **insurance brokerage industry**. Every successful team relies on clearly defined goals and a systematic evaluation of progress towards achieving those goals. How can a **leader** effectively **assess** where their team is **currently** positioned in terms of **reaching** their **targets** compared to the **set expectations**? Provide a **detailed** guide that includes **understanding** the **goals**,

setting clear KPIs, utilizing tools and techniques for tracking and monitoring, conducting regular reviews and feedback sessions, identifying areas of concern or improvement, realigning strategies or approaches if necessary, and fostering a culture of transparency, accountability, and collaboration. Include practical examples, best practices, methodologies, and resources suitable for the **nsurance brokerage industry.** Respond separately to each question. Explore unconventional solutions and alternative perspectives. Let's take this one step at a time. Write using a friendly tone and approachable writing style.

Formula

Act as a **[profession]** specializing in the **[industry]**. Every successful team relies on clearly defined goals and a systematic evaluation of progress towards achieving those goals. How can a **[leader/manager/supervisor]** effectively **[assess/evaluate/measure]** where their team is **[currently/now/presently]** positioned in terms of **[reaching/achieving/meeting]** their **[targets/objectives/aims]** compared to the **[set/established/planned]** **[expectations/benchmarks/standards]**? Provide a **[detailed/comprehensive/in-depth]** guide that includes **[understanding/knowing/getting clear on]** **[the goals/objectives/targets/vision/mission]**, **[setting/creating/establishing]** **[clear/definite/specific]** **[benchmarks/KPIs/standards/indicators]**, **[utilizing/using/applying]** **[tools and techniques/methods and approaches/systems and technology]** for **[tracking/monitoring/observing]** and **[monitoring/measuring/evaluating]**, **[conducting/organizing/holding]** **[regular/frequent/consistent]** **[reviews/feedback sessions/evaluation meetings]**, **[identifying/recognizing/pinpointing]** **[areas of concern or improvement/opportunities for growth/challenges or roadblocks]**, **[realigning/adjusting/tweaking]** **[strategies or approaches/methods or tactics/plans or directions]** if **[necessary/required/needed]**, and **[fostering/encouraging/promoting]** a **[culture/environment/atmosphere]** of **[transparency/accountability/responsibility]** and **[collaboration/cooperation/teamwork]**. Include **[practical/real-life/actual]** **[examples/scenarios/case studies]**, **[best practices/guidelines/recommendations]**, **[methodologies/techniques/processes]**, and **[resources/tools/materials]** suitable for the **[industry]**. Respond separately to each question. Explore unconventional solutions and alternative perspectives. Let's take this one step at a time. Write using a **[type]** tone and **[style]** writing style.

Examples

Example 1: Act as a Leadership Coach for a startup environment. How can a startup founder assess where their core team is currently positioned in terms of achieving quarterly growth targets compared to the set expectations? Provide a comprehensive guide that includes establishing S.M.A.R.T goals, leveraging project management tools, conducting bi-weekly review meetings, fostering an open feedback culture, and dynamically realigning strategies to match market trends. Include examples specific to startups, agile methodologies, and digital resources. Respond separately to each question. Discover rare insights and pioneering ideas. Let's unpack this topic. Write using a formal tone and concise writing style.

Example 2: Act as a Team Performance Specialist in a large corporation. How can a department manager effectively measure where their team is in reaching annual sales targets compared to planned benchmarks? Provide an in-depth guide that includes defining sales KPIs, utilizing CRM systems, conducting monthly performance evaluations, working closely with team members to address individual needs, and creating a transparent reporting structure. Include case studies from large corporate settings, standardized practices, and enterprise-level tools. Respond separately to each question. Offer extraordinary advice and non-mainstream opinions. Let's explore this subject systematically. Write using a diplomatic tone and tactful writing style.

PROMPT No 46

Tags
Team-Reflection - Motivation - Goal-Setting

Goal
To guide the team in thoughtful reflection and candid discussion about their individual and collective aspirations. This exercise aims to clarify what team members genuinely want to achieve, both for themselves and as a part of the team, thereby setting the stage for focused, purposeful work and strategy planning.

Prompt
Act as a **Motivational Coach** specializing in **goal-setting and vision alignment** for the **real estate industry**. Could you provide an **exhaustive guide** on how to **effectively conduct a team session aimed at reflecting on what each member truly desires to accomplish**?
I am particularly interested in **engaging exercises and questioning techniques that can unlock deeper levels of personal and professional desire**. The guide should be organized into into preparation, discussion facilitation, and conclusion and follow-up. Include uncommon advice and underrated resources. Let's sequentially address each element. Write using an **inspiring** tone and a **holistic** writing style.

Formula
Act as a [profession] with expertise in [specialization/topic] for the [industry]. Could you provide a [type of resource/tool] on how to [targeted goal/challenge]? I am particularly interested in [particular methods/aspects]. The guide should be organized into [sections/themes]. Include uncommon advice and underrated resources. Let's sequentially address each element. Write using a [type] tone and [style] writing style.

Examples
Example 1: Act as a Business Psychologist focused on employee engagement. Could you present a toolkit for a team reflection session centered on exploring what team members really want to achieve? I would like to emphasize methods that encourage deep emotional and psychological engagement with their goals. Include suggested activities, tips for creating a safe space for self-exploration, and practical methods for synthesizing these goals into action plans. Share distinctive guidance and unexplored options. Let's scrutinize this topic incrementally. Write using an empathetic tone and an evidence-based writing style.

Example 2: Act as a Leadership Consultant specializing in organizational purpose and culture. Could you design a framework for leading a team discussion that aims to bring clarity to what members truly want to achieve in the context of the organization's mission? I'm looking for an approach that aligns individual aspirations with the organization's broader objectives. Include question prompts, possible challenges to be aware of, and methods for integrating the outcomes of this discussion into our strategic planning. Provide a meticulous and wide-ranging response. Let's examine each dimension meticulously. Write using an empowering tone and a forward-thinking writing style.

HABITS

PROMPT No 47

Tags
Obstacles - Methodologies - Strategy

Goal

To explore and outline methodologies or strategies that can be employed to identify potential external obstacles that might obstruct the achievement of targeted deliverables. This guidance aims to help professionals anticipate challenges, adapt, and strategize accordingly to ensure that they meet their business targets.

Prompt

Act as a **Change Management Consultant** specializing in the **manufacturing industry**. What are some **crucial methodologies or strategies I should consider to identify potential external obstacles that might hinder achieving my targeted deliverables**? The intent is **to understand the external factors and to develop proactive strategies to mitigate or overcome these challenges**. Let's dissect this carefully. Write using an **analytical** tone and **technical** writing style.

Formula

Act as a [profession] specializing in the [industry]. What are some [contextual challenge/opportunity]? The intent is to [desired outcome]. Let's dissect this carefully. Write using a [type] tone and [style] writing style.

Examples

Example 1: Act as a Performance Coach specializing in the logistics industry, could you guide me through essential methodologies or strategies for identifying and navigating potential external obstacles that might disrupt achieving specific project deliverables? The goal is to align strategic planning with potential market dynamics and environmental factors. Let's analyze this piece by piece. Write using a confident tone and informative writing style.

Example 2: Act as a Risk Management Analyst specializing in the financial sector, could you outline the critical approaches or mechanisms that can be employed to recognize potential external threats or barriers that could hinder meeting our organizational goals and targets? The intention is to develop a resilient and adaptive framework for understanding and mitigating such challenges. Let's think about this step by step. Write using an authoritative tone and analytical writing style.

PROMPT No 48

Tags

Communication - ActiveListening - Self-awareness

Goal

To identify the signs, triggers, or behaviors that might indicate a lapse in active listening to team members, and to reflect on those situations or circumstances where this tends to occur. The understanding of these elements aims to promote self-awareness and improve communication within the team.

Prompt

Act as a **Communication Specialist** specializing in the **power generation industry**. Could you provide a **profound and detailed analysis of how I can recognize when I am not actively listening to my team**? Furthermore, what **methods or reflective practices can I employ to understand the specific situations where I tend to disengage from listening**? Respond separately to each question. Include both readily observable indicators and subtle signs of inattention, along with actionable strategies for self-reflection and improvement. Let's consider each facet of this topic. Write using an **instructive** tone and **engaging** writing style.

Formula

Act as a **[profession]** specializing in the **[industry]**. Could you provide **[contextual challenge/opportunity]**? Furthermore, what **[contextual challenge/opportunity]**? Respond separately to each question. Include both readily observable indicators and subtle signs of inattention, along with actionable strategies for self-reflection and improvement. Let's consider each facet of this topic. Write using a **[type]** tone and **[style]** writing style.

Examples

Example 1: Act as a Team Development Specialist specializing in the healthcare industry. Could you provide insights on how I can notice when I am not really listening to my team? Furthermore, what methods or reflective techniques can I employ to understand the specific situations where I tend to disengage from listening? Respond separately to each question. Include strategies for reflection on situations where I might tune out, and propose practical steps for enhanced listening skills. Let's unpack this topic. Write using a concise tone and constructive writing style.

Example 2: Act as a Leadership Coach specializing in the manufacturing industry. Could you deliver an all-inclusive and extensive commentary on recognizing when I'm failing to listen to my team? Furthermore, what methods or reflective practices can I employ to understand the specific situations where I tend to disengage from listening? Respond separately to each question. Include both behavioral cues and mental patterns, and guide me on reflective practices to understand and overcome this barrier. Let's dissect this carefully. Write using a professional tone and persuasive writing style.

LEARNING

PROMPT No 49

Tags

Energy - Motivation - Leadership

Goal

To recognize early signs of declining energy or motivation within a team and to explore strategic interventions to rejuvenate and increase energy and enthusiasm. The focus is on proactive leadership that fosters a vibrant and engaged team culture.

Prompt

Act as a Leadership Development Consultant specializing in the e-commerce industry. What are the symptoms or signs that the energy of my team is decreasing?, and what actionable strategies can I employ to correct this trend and increase their vitality and motivation? Respond to each question separately. Identifying and addressing these factors is vital for maintaining team productivity and morale. Provide exhaustive and all-encompassing responses. Let's analyze this piece by piece. Write using an enthusiastic tone and engaging writing style.

Formula

Act as a **[profession]** specializing in the **[industry]**. What are the symptoms or signs that **[contextual challenge/opportunity]**? And what actionable strategies can I **[contextual challenge/opportunity]**? Respond to each question separately. Identifying and addressing these factors is vital for **[desired outcome]**. Provide exhaustive and all-encompassing responses. Let's analyze this piece by piece. Write using a **[type]** tone and **[style]** writing style.

Examples

Example 1: Act as an Employee Engagement Consultant specializing in the tech industry. What are the signs that the creative energy of my development team is waning? And what innovative methods can I use to reinvigorate their passion and creativity? Respond to each question separately. Understanding and nurturing these dynamics is key to sustaining innovation and collaboration. Deliver rigorous and thoroughgoing responses. Let's consider each facet of this topic. Write using an inspired tone and creative writing style.

Example 2: Act as a Team Coach specializing in the hospitality industry. What are the symptoms that my customer service team's enthusiasm and commitment are declining? And what personalized strategies can I apply to renew their energy and dedication to excellence? Respond to each question separately. This proactive approach is essential for delivering exceptional customer experiences. Create systematic and far-reaching responses. Let's unpack this topic systematically. Write using a caring tone and informative writing style.

PROMPT No 50

Tags
Opportunities - Vigilance - Identification
Goal
To equip business leaders with a robust methodology for proactively identifying and seizing business opportunities that align with the company's strategic objectives. The focus is on creating an organizational environment that encourages vigilance, collaboration, and quick decision-making.
Prompt
Act as a **Business Opportunity Analyst** specializing in **competitive intelligence** for the **energy industry**. Could you provide a **comprehensive guide on how I can ensure my team doesn't miss a great opportunity for our business in the future**? This is crucial for **maintaining a competitive edge and achieving long-term success**. Your guide should be inclusive of techniques for opportunity identification, risk assessment, and decision-making processes. Explore unconventional solutions and alternative perspectives. Let's tackle this in a phased manner. Write using an **authoritative** tone and a **detailed, systematic** writing style.
Formula
Act as a [profession] specializing in [focus area] for the [industry]. Could you provide a [specific challenge or opportunity]? This is crucial for [desired outcome]. Your guidance should include [tactics/considerations/strategies]. Explore unconventional solutions and alternative perspectives. Let's tackle this in a phased manner. Write using a [type] tone and [style] writing style.
Examples

Example 1: Act as a Strategic Management Consultant specializing in the retail industry. Could you elucidate strategies that my team can employ to ensure we don't overlook significant market opportunities, especially during seasonal peaks? This is vital for maximizing revenue and market share. Your advice should explore methods for market analysis, trend-spotting, and quick decision-making protocols. Unearth hidden gems and non-traditional methods. Let's methodically dissect each component. Write using a persuasive tone and a data-driven writing style.

Example 2: Act as a Corporate Innovation Expert specializing in digital transformation. Could you outline a framework my IT team could use to identify and seize emerging technological opportunities that could put us ahead of the competition? This is fundamental for maintaining a cutting-edge profile in a rapidly evolving industry. Your framework should cover aspects like continuous learning, open innovation, and collaboration with external partners. Delve into uncharted territories and groundbreaking concepts. Let's scrutinize this topic incrementally. Write using an inspiring tone and an innovation-focused writing style.

PROMPT No 51

Tags

Motivation - Reflection - Positivity

Goal

To guide leaders in developing effective strategies for motivating their team to engage in reflective practices, focusing on what went well in a recent project or task. By doing so, the team can identify best practices, enhance their skills, and maintain a positive work environment.

Prompt

Act as a **Business Performance Coach** specializing in **intrinsic motivation and positive reinforcement** for the **logistics industry**. Could you provide a **comprehensive guide** on how to **incentivize my team to reflect on what worked well in a recent project**? I'd like to understand **techniques for encouraging self-reflection and group discussions that focus on the positives, thereby fostering an environment of continuous improvement and team morale**. Please include both individual and group activities, along with appropriate metrics to gauge success. Give a complete and in-depth interpretation. Let's consider each facet of this topic. Write using a **formal** tone and **concise** writing style.

Formula

Act as a **[profession]** specializing in **[focus area]** for the **[industry]**. Could you provide a **[comprehensive guide/detailed framework]** on how to **[specific challenge or opportunity]**? I'd like to understand **[sub-goals/specific techniques]**. Please include **[specific elements/additional requirements]**. Give a complete and in-depth interpretation. Let's consider each facet of this topic. Write using a formal tone and concise writing style.

Examples

Example 1: Act as a Leadership Development Consultant specializing in team dynamics and positive psychology. Could you outline a roadmap for encouraging my remote team to discuss and document what went particularly well in our latest product launch? I'd like to know how to create a psychologically safe space for this discussion to happen, even when team members are not in the same location. Please include tips for conducting effective virtual meetings, ice-breaker activities, and methods for consolidating insights. Submit a thoroughgoing and expansive review. Let's unpack this topic. Write using a professional tone and clear writing style.

Example 2: Act as an Organizational Development Specialist specializing in gamification techniques. Could you provide a step-by-step guide on how to introduce gamified elements into team reflections focused on positive outcomes in our recent sales campaign? I want to make the process engaging and fun while ensuring we capture valuable insights. Please include game ideas, scoring methods, and follow-up strategies to integrate these positive takeaways into future projects. Assemble a meticulous and wide-ranging analysis. Let's take this one step at a time. Write using a persuasive tone and argumentative writing style.

PROMPT No 52

Tags

Reflection - ProjectManagement - Self-awareness

Goal

To enable leaders to harness the momentum and positive energy generated by a successful project to foster self-awareness and continuous growth within their teams. By approaching this conversation effectively, leaders can help team members identify strengths, lessons learned, and areas for future development.

Prompt

Act as a **Professional Development Coach** specializing in **team dynamics** for the **project management industry**. Could you provide a **structured outline on how I should conduct a reflective conversation with my team about what they could learn from a recently successful project**? This is essential for **encouraging self-awareness, reinforcing strengths, and identifying areas for further growth**. Your outline should include **key talking points, appropriate timing for such discussions, and tips for encouraging an open and honest dialogue**. Offer a meticulous and expansive response. Let's tackle this in a phased manner. Write using an **encouraging** tone and an **action-oriented** writing style.

Formula

Act as a **[profession]** specializing in **[topic/specialization]** for the **[industry]**. Could you provide a **[contextual challenge/opportunity]**? This is essential for **[desired outcome]**. Your outline should include **[method/strategy/approach]**. Offer a meticulous and expansive response. Let's tackle this in a phased manner. Write using a **[type]** tone and **[style]** writing style.

Examples

Example 1: Act as a Leadership Strategist specializing in the tech industry. Could you provide a structured outline on how I should approach a conversation with my software development team regarding what they could learn from their recent success in launching a new application? This is critical for instilling a culture of continuous improvement and leveraging strengths for future projects. Your outline should include tips for setting a positive atmosphere, encouraging self-reflection, and discussing potential skill-building opportunities. Present a detailed and broad-ranging response. Let's consider each facet of this topic. Write using an analytical tone and a results-focused writing style.

Example 2: Act as an Employee Engagement Expert specializing in retail. Could you provide a comprehensive guide on how to engage my sales team in a discussion about the lessons they can glean from our record-breaking sales quarter? This is crucial for maintaining high morale and building a culture of excellence. Your guidance should cover how to acknowledge individual contributions, facilitate peer-to-peer learning, and set new benchmarks for success. Supply a detailed and holistic response. Let's take this one step at a time. Write using a motivational tone and a team-centric writing style.

PROMPT No 53

Tags

TalentDevelopment - Alignment - Interests

Goal

To understand how to identify and assess the areas or topics that team members are eager to learn about, ensuring that they are congruent with the organization's mission, values, and strategic objectives.

Prompt

Act as a **Talent Development Specialist** specializing in the **banking industry**. Could you provide **a comprehensive and elaborate depiction of how I can ascertain the subjects or fields my team is keen to explore and learn about**? Furthermore, how can I **align these interests with the company's priorities, values, and strategic direction**? Include methodologies for surveying interests, evaluating relevance, and creating a symbiotic learning plan that benefits both the team members and the organization. Let's analyze this piece by piece. Write using an **inspirational** tone and **creative** writing style.

Formula

Act as a **[profession]** specializing in the **[industry]**. Could you provide **[contextual challenge/opportunity]**? Furthermore, how can I **[contextual challenge/opportunity]**? Include methodologies for surveying interests, evaluating relevance, and creating a symbiotic learning plan that benefits both the team members and the organization. Let's analyze this piece by piece. Write using a **[type]** tone and **[style]** writing style.

Examples

Example 1: Act as a Leadership Development Consultant specializing in the technology industry. Could you share distinctive guidance and unexplored options on how to identify the learning interests of my team that are most relevant to our tech company? Include strategies for assessing interests, aligning with company goals, and fostering continuous learning. Let's think about this step by step. Write using an enthusiastic tone and informative writing style.

Example 2: Act as an Organizational Development Consultant specializing in the retail industry. Could you provide unique insights and overlooked opportunities to discover the topics my retail team wants to learn about, ensuring alignment with the company's core values and market needs? Include both conventional and innovative approaches to align learning and development with organizational strategy. Let's dissect this carefully. Write using a confident tone and analytical writing style.

PROMPT No 54

Tags
Investigation - Failure - Improvement

Goal
To gain a detailed and specific plan of action to thoroughly investigate and analyze a recent failure with a team, with the goal of identifying and learning from any mistakes made, fostering a learning culture and continuous improvement.

Prompt
Given the challenge of **learning from a recent failure**, as a **Leadership Development Facilitator** and in a **constructive and professional tone**, could you provide a detailed and specific plan of action **I** can use to thoroughly investigate and analyze **this experience** with **my team**, with the goal of **identifying and learning from any mistakes made**?

Formula
Given the challenge of **[contextual challenge/opportunity]**, as a **[profession]** and in a **[tone of voice]**, could you provide a detailed and specific plan of action **[I/Name/Role]** can use to thoroughly investigate and analyze **[specific situation]** with **[my/their] [team/group/department]**, with the goal of **[desired outcome]**?

Examples
Example 1: Given the challenge of learning from a recent product launch failure, as a Business Coach and in a respectful and solution-oriented tone, could you provide a detailed and specific plan of action project manager can use to thoroughly investigate and analyze this experience with their team, with the goal of identifying and learning from any mistakes made?

Example 2: As a Performance Coach, in a supportive and clear tone, could you provide a detailed and specific plan of action I can use to thoroughly investigate and analyze a recent project failure with my engineering team, with the goal of identifying and learning from any mistakes made? This advice is particularly relevant given the challenge of learning from a recent failure.

PROMPT No 55

Tags
Learning - Reflection - Actionability

Goal
To create a constructive learning environment where team members can openly reflect on situations they wish they had handled differently, fostering personal and professional growth. The objective is to provide a framework that not only facilitates honest discussion but also leads to actionable insights for future improvement.

Prompt
Act as an **Organizational Learning Expert** specializing in **reflective practices**. Could you provide a **comprehensive guide** on how to **lead my team in learning from situations where they wish they had acted differently**? I'm particularly interested in **methods to encourage open dialogue, psychological techniques to reduce defensive behavior, and activities to promote reflection and learning**. Break down the guide into

pre-session planning, during the session, and follow-up activities for sustained learning. Investigate unexpected avenues and creative pathways. Let's unpack this topic. Write using a **supportive** tone and an **insightful** writing style.

Formula

Act as a [profession] specializing in [specialized area]. Could you provide a [guide/resources] on how to [specific challenge/opportunity]? I'm particularly interested in [particular elements/techniques]. Break down the guide into pre-session planning, during the session, and follow-up activities for sustained learning. Investigate unexpected avenues and creative pathways. Let's unpack this topic. Write using a [specified tone] and [writing style].

Examples

Example 1: Act as a Behavioral Psychologist with a focus on team dynamics. Could you supply a detailed guide on fostering an atmosphere where my team can openly discuss and learn from their past actions they regret? I'd like to explore strategies that utilize behavioral psychology to promote self-awareness and accountability. Include activities that can be incorporated into team meetings, specific question prompts, and a plan for ongoing reflection. Suggest fresh approaches and inventive strategies. Let's take this one step at a time. Write using an empathetic tone and a constructive writing style.

Example 2: Act as a Leadership Coach specializing in vulnerability and trust. Could you outline a guide on how to use vulnerability as a tool to help my team discuss situations where they wish they had acted differently? I'd like the guide to focus on building trust to make these difficult conversations more effective. Please provide suggestions for ice-breakers, methods for sharing experiences without judgment, and actionable steps for implementing learnings. Discover rare insights and pioneering ideas. Let's think about this step by step. Write using a nurturing tone and an empowering writing style.

LISTENING

PROMPT No 56

Tags

Performance-Enhancement - Conversation - Improvement

Goal

To facilitate a constructive conversation among team members about missed opportunities stemming from subpar performance. The objective is to help the team identify what led to these missed opportunities and develop strategies for improvement, thereby contributing to both personal and team growth

Prompt

Act as a **Performance Enhancement Expert** specializing in **learning from setbacks**. Could you provide **a detailed guide** on how to **initiate and lead conversations with my team about the opportunities they've missed due to not performing at their best**? I am particularly interested in **establishing a safe space for these discussions, using evidence-based methods to guide the conversation, and formulating actionable steps for avoiding similar issues in the future**. Divide the guide into sections addressing the preparation, execution, and follow-up of these conversations. Offer extraordinary advice and non-mainstream opinions. Let's unpack this topic. Write using a **respectful** tone and a **solution-oriented** writing style.

Formula

Act as a **[profession]** specializing in **[specialized area]**. Could you provide a **[type of guide/resource]** on how to **[specific challenge/opportunity]**? I am particularly interested in **[particular elements/techniques]**. Divide the guide into sections addressing the preparation, execution, and follow-up of these conversations. Offer extraordinary advice and non-mainstream opinions. Let's unpack this topic. Write using a **[specified tone]** and **[specified writing style]**.

Examples

Example 1: Act as an Organizational Psychologist focusing on psychological safety. Could you offer a blueprint on how to create a safe and welcoming environment in which team members can discuss missed opportunities arising from not being at their best? I'd like to incorporate methods that encourage psychological safety, empathy, and mutual respect into these discussions. Include techniques for setting the atmosphere, opening the conversation, and promoting open dialogue. Reveal lesser-known practices and innovative techniques. Let's take this one step at a time. Write using an inclusive tone and a comprehensive writing style.

Example 2: Act as a Business Coach with expertise in team dynamics and problem-solving. Could you outline a strategy for facilitating team meetings aimed at dissecting missed opportunities due to suboptimal performance? I am looking for a structured format that helps identify the root causes, explore alternative actions, and establishes a plan for future situations. Include checklists, exercises, and potential pitfalls to avoid. Highlight imaginative thoughts and avant-garde solutions. Let's think about this step by step. Write using a constructive tone and an actionable writing style.

PROMPT No 57

Tags

Resilience - Mindfulness - Strategy

Goal

To provide targeted strategies to a team so that they can prevent minor issues from affecting their performance and morale in the future. This inquiry focuses on resilience, proactive problem-solving, and mindfulness within a specific industry setting.

Prompt

Act as a **Team Development Specialist** specializing in the **manufacturing industry**. What are some **comprehensive and effective strategies I can share with my team to enable them to avert the influence of minor issues on their future performance and morale**? These strategies should foster resilience, mindfulness, and proactive problem-solving. The goal is to **improve overall team robustness and emotional intelligence**. Let's dissect this carefully. Write using an **encouraging** tone and **engaging** writing style.

Formula

Act as a **[profession]** specializing in the **[industry]**. What are some **[contextual challenge/opportunity]**? These strategies should foster resilience, mindfulness, and proactive problem-solving. The goal is to **[goal]**. Let's dissect this carefully. Write using a **[type]** tone and **[style]** writing style.

Examples

Example 1: Act as a Leadership Coach specializing in the finance industry, could you provide unique insights and strategies that I can share with my team to prevent minor setbacks or issues from impacting their future productivity and job satisfaction? The goal is to enhance mental resilience and manage stress effectively. Let's analyze this piece by piece. Write using an inspirational tone and creative writing style.

Example 2: Act as a Performance Coach specializing in the education sector, could you propose a comprehensive and elaborate depiction of techniques and approaches I can relay to my team to assist them in avoiding the interference of small hindrances or challenges on their future achievements? The goal is to foster emotional intelligence and adaptability within the team. Let's think about this step by step. Write using a motivated tone and conversational writing style.

MINDSET

PROMPT No 58

Tags
Leadership - Transparency - Accountability

Goal
To enhance preparedness in having candid conversations with team members regarding their individual successes or failures and the implications of these outcomes on their roles, contributions to the team, and alignment with company goals. The ultimate objective is to foster transparency, encourage personal accountability, facilitate growth, and cultivate a shared understanding of performance standards and expectations.

Prompt
Act as a **Leadership Development Coach** specializing in the **food & beverage manufacturing**. Could you guide me through the process of **effectively preparing to have sincere conversations with my team about what their success or failure means, in terms of work and contribution to the team and company**? This involves **understanding individual perceptions, recognizing performance metrics, communicating expectations, and facilitating reflective dialogue**. Please provide a thorough framework, including **preparation strategies, communication techniques, emotional intelligence insights, and follow-up actions**. Produce a sweeping and meticulous response. Let's analyze this from multiple angles. Write using an **encouraging** tone and **insightful** writing style.

Formula
Act as a [profession] specializing in the [industry]. Could you guide me through the process of [contextual challenge/opportunity]? This involves [desired outcome]. Please provide a thorough framework, including [specific components or methods]. Produce a sweeping and meticulous response. Let's analyze this from multiple angles. Write using a [type] tone and [style] writing style.

Examples

Example 1: Act as an Employee Engagement Consultant specializing in the tech industry. Could you guide me through the process of preparing to discuss with my engineers what their recent project success or failure means, in terms of technical growth and alignment with our team's innovation goals? This encompasses analyzing performance data, defining success parameters, acknowledging individual contributions, and devising future development plans. Please outline a compassionate and actionable approach, factoring in technical competencies, motivational factors, feedback techniques, and ongoing support mechanisms. Extend a detailed and exhaustive response. Let's handle this with care and clarity. Write using an empathetic tone and analytical writing style.

Example 2: Act as a Team Dynamics Specialist specializing in the healthcare sector. Could you guide me through the process of preparing to have an open conversation with my nursing staff about what their clinical successes or challenges mean, in terms of patient care and alignment with our unit's mission? This involves recognizing clinical outcomes, appreciating teamwork, aligning with ethical standards, and fostering continuous learning. Please develop a human-centered and reflective method, encompassing clinical standards, team collaboration, ethical considerations, and professional growth pathways. Provide a meticulous and wide-ranging response. Let's approach this with respect and thoughtfulness. Write using an inspiring tone and engaging writing style.

PROMPT No 59

Tags
Vulnerability - Well-being - Psychological-Safety
Goal
To equip team leaders, managers, and executives with the tools and strategies to identify conditions where their team feels most vulnerable at work. Understanding these aspects is crucial for optimizing team performance, mental health, and long-term job satisfaction.
Prompt
Act as an **Organizational Well-being Specialist** specializing in **psychological safety and employee wellness** for the **retail industry**. Could you guide me through **the methods to discover what conditions make my team feel most vulnerable at work**? I'm also interested in creating a framework to improve overall well-being within my team. Please provide a **step-by-step guide** to improve the psychological landscape of my team. Suggest actionable strategies to address discovered vulnerabilities and improve the team's sense of safety and well-being. Explore unconventional solutions and alternative perspectives. Let's tackle this request comprehensively. Write using a **nurturing** tone and an **empathetic** writing style.
Formula
Act as a [profession] specializing in [topic/specialization] for the [industry]. Could you guide me through [contextual challenge/opportunity]? I'm also interested in creating a framework to improve overall well-being within my team. Please provide a [step-by-step guide/questionnaires/tools/strategy] to improve the psychological landscape of my team. Explore unconventional solutions and alternative perspectives. Let's tackle this request comprehensively. Write using a [type] tone and [style] writing style.
Examples
Example 1: Act as a Mental Health Consultant specializing in workplace stress and burnout for the tech industry. Could you guide me through uncovering the factors that contribute to my team's sense of vulnerability? I'd like to focus on setting up a wellness program that addresses these specific concerns. Provide strategies to create a culture of openness and psychological safety. Include uncommon advice and underrated resources. Let's approach this holistically. Write using a supportive tone and a detail-oriented writing style.
Example 2: Act as an Employee Engagement Expert specializing in team morale for the hospitality industry. Could you help me understand the scenarios or conditions where my staff feels most uneasy or vulnerable? I aim to develop a series of team-building activities designed to fortify emotional resilience. Share a structured approach, relevant surveys, and key performance indicators to monitor improvement. Provide unique insights and overlooked opportunities. Let's delve into this deeply. Write using an uplifting tone and a thorough writing style.

PROMPT No 60

Tags
Talent - Identification - Delegation

Goal
To guide team leaders in identifying the unique qualities, strengths, and talents of each team member. Doing so allows for more tailored coaching, better delegation, and a more cohesive, effective team environment.

Prompt
Act as a **Talent Identification Specialist** specializing in the **technology sector**. Could you lay out **a comprehensive methodology for discovering what is unique about each of my software engineers**? This should include **assessment techniques, observation strategies, and conversation prompts** that can help me to pinpoint each team member's unique qualities. This is crucial for **effective team management and individual development**. Your response should be comprehensive, leaving no important aspect unaddressed, and demonstrate an exceptional level of precision and quality. Let's think about this step by step. Write using an **analytical** tone and an **instructive** writing style.

Formula
Act as a [profession] specializing in [industry]. Could you lay out [contextual challenge/opportunity]? This should include [tools/techniques]. This is crucial for [desired objectives]. Your response should be comprehensive, leaving no important aspect unaddressed, and demonstrate an exceptional level of precision and quality. Let's think about this step by step. Write using a [type] tone and [style] writing style.

Examples
Example 1: Act as an HR Consultant specializing in the healthcare industry. Could you outline a step-by-step methodology for identifying what is unique about each of my nurses and medical staff? Include relevant assessment tools, key behavioral indicators to observe, and sample questions to ask during one-on-ones. This is essential for optimizing the distribution of tasks and for individual professional growth. Explore unconventional solutions and alternative perspectives. Let's examine each part closely. Write using a compassionate tone and an evidence-based writing style.

Example 2: Act as a Team Dynamics Expert specializing in the retail sector. Could you provide a comprehensive guide for discovering what makes each of my sales associates unique? The guide should cover personality assessments, observational criteria, and topics to explore during team meetings or one-on-one sessions. This is vital for maximizing sales performance and employee satisfaction. Examine overlooked possibilities and imaginative routes. Let's delve into each aspect. Write using an engaging tone and a practical writing style.

PROMPT No 61

Tags
Transparency - Role-Clarity - Objectives

Goal
To equip leaders with a comprehensive guide for conducting conversations with team members about their current objectives and roles within the team. The aim is to foster a culture of transparency, alignment, and engagement, encouraging team members to take ownership of their responsibilities and align their individual goals with the team's broader objectives.

Prompt

Act as an **Executive Coach** specializing in **Role Clarity and Team Alignment** for the **real estate development industry**. Could you provide an **exhaustive guide** on how to **lead a conversation with my team to discuss their current objectives and their roles within the team**? I am particularly interested in **techniques that will make team members comfortable in opening up about their personal and professional goals**. Include a variety of question prompts, interactive exercises, and perhaps even digital tools that can facilitate this discussion. Divide the guide into **key phases such as preparation, the actual conversation, and post-discussion actions**. Present novel interpretations and visionary possibilities. Let's analyze this piece by piece. Write using a **reflective** tone and **thoughtful** writing style.

Formula

Act as a [profession] specializing in [expertise/topic] for the [industry]. Could you provide a [comprehensive guide/methodology] on how to [contextual challenge/opportunity]? I am particularly interested in [specific techniques/areas of focus]. Include [question prompts/interactive exercises/digital tools]. Divide the guide into [specific phases/sections]. Present novel interpretations and visionary possibilities. Let's analyze this piece by piece. Write using a [type] tone and [style] writing style.

Examples

Example 1: Act as a Communications Specialist focusing on Internal Team Dynamics for the automotive manufacturing industry. Could you produce a detailed guide on how to conduct a dialogue with my software engineering team about their current project objectives and how they view their roles in achieving them? I want to use this discussion to identify any misalignments and correct them early. Incorporate open-ended question prompts, role-playing exercises, and visualization techniques. Segment the guide into preparation, opening the conversation, deep dive, and closing with actionable items. Probe into nonconformist solutions and divergent viewpoints. Let's dissect this carefully. Write using a neutral tone and unbiased writing style.

Example 2: Act as a Leadership Development Coach specializing in Employee Engagement. Could you provide a comprehensive guide on initiating a conversation with my marketing team about their quarterly goals and their specific roles in achieving these? I'm particularly interested in employing emotional intelligence frameworks to ease the team into sharing openly. Include both group activities and individual reflection exercises, and suggest digital tools for anonymous feedback. Structure the guide into sections such as setting the environment, initiating the conversation, deep discussion, and conclusion with actionable insights. Excavate untapped resources and unconventional tactics. Let's break this down into manageable parts. Write using a reflective tone and thoughtful writing style.

OPTIONS

PROMPT No 62

Tags

Proactive - Collaboration - Bankruptcy

Goal

To catalyze a proactive, collaborative, and innovative mindset among the team, enabling them to devise robust strategies and choices to navigate potential bankruptcy or economic crises, ensuring business continuity and resilience.

Prompt

Act as a **Crisis Management Strategist** specializing in **Financial Resilience** within the **retail industry**. Could you guide me through **a structured approach to ignite my team's proactive thinking and collaborative effort in devising choices for navigating a potential bankruptcy or economic crisis**? Please include **brainstorming techniques, scenario planning, and financial analysis tools**. Make sure to cover how **to foster a conducive environment for open discussion and innovative thinking**. Delve into unconventional solutions and emerging best practices that could provide a fresh perspective on crisis management. Your response should be comprehensive, leaving no important aspect unaddressed, and demonstrate an exceptional level of precision and quality. Let's think about this step by step. Write using an **empowering** tone and a **detailed, instructional** writing style.

Formula

Act as a **[profession]** specializing in **[area of expertise]** within the **[industry]**. Could you guide me through **[specific challenge/opportunity]**? Please include **[methods/techniques]**. Make sure to cover how **[key areas/topics]**. Delve into unconventional solutions and emerging best practices that could provide a fresh perspective on crisis management. Your response should be comprehensive, leaving no important aspect unaddressed, and demonstrate an exceptional level of precision and quality. Let's think about this step by step. Write using a **[type]** tone and a **[style]** writing style.

Examples

Example 1: Act as a Financial Resilience Coach specializing in Crisis Mitigation within the manufacturing sector. Could you guide me through inspiring my team to collaboratively come up with viable options to weather a potential bankruptcy or economic downturn? Please include risk assessment tools, financial forecasting, and innovative problem-solving techniques. Make sure to cover how to create a psychologically safe space for candid discussion and brainstorming. Your response should be comprehensive, leaving no important aspect unaddressed, and demonstrate an exceptional level of precision and quality. Let's think about this step by step. Write using an engaging tone and a structured, instructional writing style.

Example 2: Act as a Bankruptcy Avoidance Advisor specializing in Proactive Financial Planning within the hospitality sector. Could you guide me through a process to activate my team's innovative and collaborative capacities in formulating strategies for averting potential bankruptcy or navigating an economic crisis? Please include contingency planning frameworks, financial literacy workshops, and cross-functional brainstorming sessions. Make sure to cover how to encourage diverse perspectives and ideas. Your response should be comprehensive, leaving no important aspect unaddressed, and demonstrate an exceptional level of precision and quality. Let's think about this step by step. Write using a forward-thinking tone and an actionable, instructional writing style.

PROMPT No 63

Tags

Resilience - Challenge-Management - Personal-Growth

Goal

To identify and explore common blind spots and biases that leaders may possess and to present strategies for recognizing and overcoming them. This information will serve to enhance self-awareness, promote inclusive leadership, and foster a more effective decision-making process.

Prompt

Act as a **Leadership Development Expert** specializing in **identifying and addressing biases within leadership roles** for the **consulting industry**. Could you explore **some common blind spots that are often persistent with**

leaders and present strategies to recognize and deal with those biases? This includes **reflecting on personal tendencies and systematic biases in decision-making**. Provide both established insights and innovative perspectives to **aid in personal and professional growth**. Let's analyze this step by step. Write using an **insightful** tone and **reflective** writing style.

Formula

Act as a [profession] specializing in [specific focus] for the [industry]. Could you explore [contextual challenge/opportunity]? This includes [additional specifications]. Provide both established insights and innovative perspectives to [desired outcome]. Let's analyze this [approach]. Write using a [type] tone and [style] writing style.

Examples

Example 1: Act as an Organizational Psychologist specializing in leadership blind spots for the non-profit industry. Could you identify common blind spots in senior management roles and offer practical solutions to recognize and overcome these biases? This includes both cognitive biases and cultural biases that may affect decision-making. Provide both time-tested strategies and cutting-edge research insights to enhance leadership effectiveness. Let's dissect this intricately. Write using an analytical tone and evidence-based writing style.

Example 2: Act as a Leadership Mentor specializing in executive coaching for the environmental consulting industry. Could you delve into the unseen barriers that often plague new entrepreneurs and suggest targeted approaches to identify and mitigate those biases? This includes an examination of personal assumptions, values, and unconscious biases that may hinder progress. Provide both classical leadership wisdom and modern empathetic approaches to foster more adaptable and conscious leadership. Let's explore this progressively. Write using an empathetic tone and inspirational writing style.

PROMPT No 64

Tags

Decision-making - Frameworks - Participation

Goal

To equip leaders with a comprehensive toolkit for effectively discussing various options with their team regarding specific decisions that need to be made at work. The aim is to facilitate informed decision-making, encourage team participation, and build consensus.

Prompt

Act as a **Decision-Making Facilitator** specializing in the **retail industry**. Could you **provide** a **structured** approach for discussing **various** options that **appeal to my team** concerning a **specific** decision they need to **make** at work? Include **frameworks** for **decision analysis, techniques for eliciting team input, and methods for achieving consensus**. Let's systematically explore each facet. Explore unconventional solutions and alternative perspectives. Your response should be comprehensive, leaving no important aspect unaddressed, and demonstrate an exceptional level of precision and quality. Write using a consultative tone and an advisory writing style.

Formula

Act as a [profession] specializing in the [industry]. Could you [provide/outline/delineate] a [structured/applicable/effective] approach for discussing [various/multiple/different] options that [appeal to/resonate with] [my/our/the] team concerning a [specific/particular/targeted] decision they need to

[make/arrive at/decide] at work? Include [frameworks/techniques/methods] for [decision analysis/team input/achieving consensus].
Let's systematically explore each facet. Explore unconventional solutions and alternative perspectives. Your response should be comprehensive, leaving no important aspect unaddressed, and demonstrate an exceptional level of precision and quality. Write using a [type] tone and [style] writing style.

Examples

Example 1: Act as a Leadership Development Coach specializing in the healthcare industry. Could you outline an effective approach for discussing multiple options that resonate with my nursing team concerning a specific scheduling decision they need to make? Include the "Decision Matrix" framework, techniques for anonymous voting, and methods for conflict resolution. Let's carefully evaluate each segment. Write using a facilitative tone and a collaborative writing style. Unearth hidden gems and non-traditional methods. Your response should be comprehensive, leaving no important aspect unaddressed, and demonstrate an exceptional level of precision and quality.

Example 2: Act as a Team Dynamics Expert specializing in the software development industry. Could you provide a structured approach for discussing various options that appeal to my development team concerning a specific technology stack decision they need to make? Include the "SWOT Analysis" framework, techniques for open brainstorming, and methods for weighted voting. Let's examine each dimension meticulously. Investigate unexpected avenues and creative pathways. Write using an analytical tone and a detailed writing style. Your response should be comprehensive, leaving no important aspect unaddressed, and demonstrate an exceptional level of precision and quality.

PERFORMANCE

PROMPT No 65

Tags
Adaptability - Growth - Accounting

Goal
To equip leaders with strategies and insights to encourage team members to step out of their comfort zones, highlighting the unforeseen benefits that can be achieved through this process. This will foster personal and professional growth, increase adaptability, and enhance creativity within the team.

Prompt
Act as a **Leadership Development Specialist** specializing in **fostering growth and adaptability** for the **accounting industry**. Could you guide me through the process of **bringing to my team's attention the unforeseen benefits they could experience by stepping outside of their comfort zones**? What are the **initial steps they can take to start this journey**? Respond separately to each question. Include both **conventional wisdom and innovative strategies in your responses**. Provide specific examples and actionable insights to motivate and inspire action. Let's examine this **methodically**. Write using an **encouraging** tone and a **motivational** writing style.

Formula
Act as a [profession] specializing in [specific focus] for the [industry]. Could you guide me through the process of [contextual challenge/opportunity]? What are the [specific requirements]? Respond separately to each question. Include both [additional specifications]. Provide [desired outcome]. Let's examine this [approach]. Write using a [type] tone and [style] writing style.

Examples

Example 1: Act as a Team Growth Coach specializing in innovation and creativity for the auditing industry. Could you help me show my team the hidden advantages they could gain by embracing new challenges and stepping outside their usual routines? What are the essential tools and mindsets they need to begin? Include both tried-and-true methods and avant-garde techniques in your response. Provide specific case studies and hands-on exercises to spark curiosity and courage. Let's explore this thoughtfully. Write using a stimulating tone and a dynamic writing style.

Example 2: Act as a Change Management Consultant specializing in organizational transformation for the legal services industry. Could you assist me in inspiring my team to recognize the unexpected rewards of pushing their boundaries and trying new approaches? What are the foundational steps and support systems required to facilitate this shift? Include both traditional leadership principles and groundbreaking behavioral science insights in your response. Provide a roadmap with checkpoints and self-assessment tools to ensure ongoing development. Let's analyze this systematically. Write using an informative tone and an engaging writing style.

PROMPT No 66

Tags

Mindset - Transformation - Support

Goal

To explore various strategies, techniques, and approaches that you can utilize to facilitate personal change and growth, leading to better results or performance in professional and personal aspects of life. This includes understanding your strengths and weaknesses, setting clear and achievable goals, embracing change, and utilizing support systems.

Prompt

Act as a **Personal Growth Coach** specializing in the **biotechnology industry**. The path to **achieving desired** results **often** requires **personal change**. What are some **fundamental** mindset shifts that professionals must **consider** to **facilitate** personal change leading to **improved performance**? How can **embracing change** contribute to **lasting** transformation? Provide **step-by-step guidelines** showcasing how **I** can **implement** these mindset shifts. Offer unconventional tips and lesser-known insights. Let's take this one step at a time. Write using a motivational tone and inspiring writing style.

Formula

Act as a [profession] specializing in the [industry]. The path to [achieving/accomplishing/attaining] [desired/better/optimal] results [often/usually/frequently] requires [personal change/adaptation/transformation]. What are some [fundamental/key/essential] [strategies/tools/mindset shifts] that [professionals/individuals/employees] must [consider/adopt/implement] to [facilitate/nurture/encourage] personal change leading to [improved/enhanced/increased] [results/performance/outcomes]? How can [list of factors such as understanding oneself, setting clear goals], contribute to [lasting/enduring/sustainable] transformation? Provide [practical examples/guidelines/scenarios] showcasing how [individuals at various career stages/different backgrounds/unique situations] can [implement/apply/use] these strategies. Offer unconventional tips and lesser-known insights. Let's take this one step at a time. Write with a [supportive/encouraging/inspiring] tone and an [analytical/thoughtful/comprehensive] writing style.

Examples

Example 1: Act as a Performance Coach specializing in the banking industry, achieving optimal results often requires a willingness to change and adapt. What are some key strategies, such as self-reflection, SMART goal setting, embracing feedback, and developing resilience, that banking professionals must consider to facilitate personal change leading to enhanced performance? How can mentorship, continuous learning, and a growth mindset contribute to positive transformations in a competitive banking environment? Provide step-by-step guidelines showcasing how banking professionals, from entry-level to executives, can implement these change-facilitating strategies. Share unexpected advice and hidden gems. Let's think about this step by step. Write using an optimistic tone and positive writing style.

Example 2: Act as a Leadership Development Consultant specializing in the tech industry, attaining desired outcomes in a rapidly changing field requires continuous personal growth. What are some essential tools and mindset shifts, like adaptability, lifelong learning, seeking diverse perspectives, and regular self-assessment, that tech leaders must adopt to nurture personal change? How does understanding individual strengths and weaknesses, setting clear career trajectories, and building supportive networks lead to innovative thinking and improved results in tech? Provide practical scenarios illustrating how these strategies can be applied by tech professionals at various stages of their career. Give atypical strategies and less recognized insights. Let's consider each aspect in detail. Write using a constructive tone and solution-focused writing style.

PROMPT No 67

Tags
Goal-Attainment - Modification - Performance
Goal
To gain insights on specific steps to accurately identify areas requiring improvement or modification, enhancing a team's ability to successfully attain their performance objectives.
Prompt
In the context of **achieving performance objectives**, as a **Performance Coach** and in a **clear and concise tone**, could you outline the specific steps that can be taken to accurately identify the areas that require improvement or modification in order for **my team** to successfully attain their **goals**?
Formula
In the context of [contextual challenge/opportunity], as a [profession] and in a [tone of voice], could you outline the specific steps that can be taken to accurately identify the areas that require improvement or modification in order for [I/Name/Role]'s [team/group/department] to successfully attain their [desired outcome]?
Examples

Example 1: In the context of achieving quarterly financial targets, as a Management Consultant and in a professional and solution-oriented tone, could you outline the specific steps that a finance manager can take to accurately identify the areas that require improvement or modification in order for their team to successfully attain their targets?

Example 2: As a Talent Development Specialist, in a supportive and respectful tone, could you outline the specific steps that can be taken to accurately identify the areas that require improvement or modification in order for my customer service team to successfully attain their customer satisfaction goals? This advice is particularly relevant in the context of improving customer service delivery.

PREFERENCES

PROMPT No 68

Tags
Rapport - Creativity - Engagement

Goal
To equip leaders and managers with the understanding and tools necessary to discern what their team members are focusing on outside their primary responsibilities. This awareness can enhance communication, foster empathy, and leverage these interests to create a more engaging and innovative work environment.

Prompt
Act as a **Work-Life Balance Expert** specializing in the **software development industry**. Could you guide me through **the techniques and approaches to discover what my team members are paying attention to besides their regular work**? This includes **hobbies, side projects, passions, or other interests**. Recognizing these aspects is essential for **building rapport, encouraging creativity, and connecting these interests to organizational goals where possible**. Please provide a comprehensive and nuanced guide, including various strategies like **one-on-one conversations, interest surveys, team-building activities, and observation techniques**. Let's explore this systematically. Write using an **empathetic** tone and **engaging** writing style.

Formula
Act as a [profession] specializing in the [industry]. Could you guide me through [contextual challenge/opportunity]? This includes [specific factors or elements]. Recognizing these aspects is essential for [desired outcome]. Please provide a comprehensive and nuanced guide, including various strategies like [methods or tools]. Let's explore this [approach]. Write using a [type] tone and [style] writing style.

Examples
Example 1: Act as a Team Engagement Specialist specializing in the marketing industry. Could you assist me in identifying what my marketing team is engaged with outside of their day-to-day tasks? This might encompass creative hobbies, volunteer work, educational pursuits, or entrepreneurial endeavors. Understanding these interests is key to enhancing team cohesion, boosting morale, and potentially sparking innovative ideas. Please detail an all-inclusive and considerate approach, utilizing techniques such as informal chats, group discussions, interest inventories, and social media analysis. Let's approach this with curiosity. Write using a conversational tone and encouraging writing style.

Example 2: Act as an Organizational Psychologist specializing in the education sector. Could you help me discover what my faculty members are concentrating on beyond their teaching and administrative duties? This may involve research projects, advocacy work, artistic pursuits, or community engagement. Gaining insight into these passions is vital for supporting their professional development, creating a more fulfilled team, and finding alignment with institutional values. Please craft a sensitive and multifaceted method, encompassing formal interviews, anonymous surveys, team workshops, and observational studies. Let's examine this thoughtfully. Write using a respectful tone and reflective writing style.

PRIORITIES

PROMPT No 69

Tags

Productivity - Diagnostics - Behavior Analysis

Goal

To obtain a holistic, actionable guide on methods for identifying actions or behaviors that need to be discontinued in order to enhance team productivity, with the aim of fostering a more efficient and effective work environment.

Prompt

As an **Organizational Psychologist** in the **technology sector**, could you provide an exhaustive guide outlining the methods **my team** and I can employ to identify actions or behaviors we need to stop doing **to increase our productivity**? Please include **both diagnostic assessments and observational techniques**. Segment the guide into **distinct categories**, and substantiate each with **empirical data and scholarly references**. Explore unconventional approaches and diverse viewpoints. Let's scrutinize this topic incrementally. Write using an **analytical** tone and a **structured** writing style.

Formula

As a [profession] in the [industry], could you provide an exhaustive guide outlining the methods [I/Name/Role] and [my/our/their] [team/group/department] can employ to identify actions or behaviors we need to stop doing to [desired outcome]? Please include both [diagnostic assessments/observational techniques]. Segment the guide into [distinct categories], and substantiate each with [empirical data/scholarly references]. Explore unconventional approaches and diverse viewpoints. Let's scrutinize this topic incrementally. Write using a [type] tone and [style] writing style.

Examples

Example 1: As a Productivity Consultant in the healthcare industry, could you provide an exhaustive guide outlining the methods a nursing team and their manager can employ to identify actions or behaviors they need to stop doing to improve patient care? Please include both self-assessment tools and peer reviews. Divide the guide into key areas, and validate each with clinical studies and peer-reviewed articles. Investigate unexpected avenues and creative pathways. Let's examine each dimension meticulously. Write using a focused tone and a concise writing style.

Example 2: As a Leadership Development Consultant in the manufacturing sector, could you provide an exhaustive guide outlining the methods my assembly line team and I can employ to identify actions or behaviors we need to stop doing to increase production efficiency? Please include both time-tracking software and team feedback mechanisms. Break the guide into actionable steps, and corroborate each with industry benchmarks and case studies. Unearth hidden gems and non-traditional methods. Let's tackle this in a phased manner. Write using a balanced tone and a nuanced writing style.

PROMPT No 70

Tags

Strategy - Decision-Making - Prioritization

Goal

To provide leaders, managers, and professionals with a robust set of strategies to identify and select key priorities to focus on. This encompasses the integration of various methodologies, decision-making frameworks, personal and organizational considerations, and balance between short-term and long-term goals.

Prompt

Act as a **Strategic Planning Expert** specializing in **corporate decision-making** for the **asset management industry**. Could you provide **a multifaceted overview of the strategies, tools, and thought processes one should consider when selecting the key priorities to focus on**? This includes **an analysis of organizational goals, personal strengths, market trends, opportunity costs, and alignment with overall strategy**. Provide nuanced insights and actionable recommendations. Let's dissect this methodically. Write using an **analytical** tone and a **structured** writing style.

Formula

Act as a [profession] specializing in [specific focus]. Could you provide [contextual challenge/opportunity]? This includes [specific requirements]. Provide nuanced insights and actionable recommendations. Let's dissect this methodically. Write using a [type] tone and [style] writing style.

Examples

Example 1: Act as a Leadership Coach specializing in small business development. Could you articulate the strategies a small business owner should consider when choosing the essential priorities to focus on for business growth? This includes understanding target audiences, evaluating resources, setting SMART goals, and balancing short-term needs with long-term vision. Provide actionable guidelines, industry-specific insights, and cautionary notes. Let's explore this step by step. Write using a motivational tone and a pragmatic writing style.

Example 2: Act as a Performance Consultant specializing in multinational corporations. Could you elaborate on the methodologies that executives in a multinational setting could implement to pinpoint the critical priorities that align with the global strategy? This includes corporate alignment, market analysis, cultural considerations, stakeholder expectations, and risk assessment. Provide tailored solutions, overlooked opportunities, and potential pitfalls. Let's analyze this systematically. Write using a confident tone and an insightful writing style.

PROGRESS

PROMPT No 71

Tags

Recognition - Morale - Engagement

Goal

To provide business leaders with a detailed strategy for initiating and conducting conversations that meaningfully celebrate team successes. The objective is to enhance the team's motivation and morale, reinforce the importance of high-quality work, and improve overall team cohesion and performance.

Prompt

Act as a **Leadership Coach** with a specialization in **Employee Engagement** for the **tech industry**, could you guide me through **how I can celebrate my team's successes in a meaningful manner that reinforces the importance of high-quality work**? Please include **methods for recognizing achievements, types of rewards** that resonate, and communication strategies to make the team feel genuinely appreciated. Make sure to cover how **the celebration can be leveraged to encourage further high-quality work**. Navigate through unexplored realms and revolutionary paradigms. Let's dissect this in a structured manner. Write using an **inspiring** tone and **engaging** writing style.

Formula

Act as a **[profession]** with a specialization in **[area of expertise]** for the **[industry]**, could you guide me through **[specific challenge/opportunity]**? Please include **[methods/techniques]**. Make sure to cover how **[key areas/topics]**. Navigate through unexplored realms and revolutionary paradigms. Let's dissect this in a structured manner. Write using a **[type]** tone and **[style]** writing style.

Examples

Example 1: Act as a Human Resources Manager with a specialization in Organizational Psychology for the healthcare industry, could you guide me through strategies for celebrating team successes that not only boost morale but also enhance focus on patient care quality? Include guidelines on choosing appropriate rewards, setting the scene for the celebration, and tailoring the message for maximum impact. Make sure to cover how such celebrations can serve as a motivational tool for sustained patient care quality. Delve into uncharted territories and groundbreaking concepts. Let's examine this step-by-step, write using a compassionate tone and clear writing style.

Example 2: Act as a Team Development Coach with a specialization in Intrinsic Motivation for the e-commerce industry, could you walk me through how to establish a culture where celebrating successes becomes an integral part of our operations? Please include tips on making these celebrations more than just a one-off event, and strategies for linking rewards to specific KPIs. Make sure to cover how these practices can drive long-term high performance. Probe into nonconformist solutions and divergent viewpoints. Let's dissect this carefully, write using an analytical tone and systematic writing style.

PROMPT No 72

Tags

Reflection - Self-awareness - Goals

Goal

To help individuals or teams in reflecting on and assessing their feelings about their progress towards specific goals or targets, enhancing self-awareness and leading to informed future actions.

Prompt

As a **Performance Coach** specializing in the **risk management industry**. Could you guide me through the process of assessing **how I feel about my progress toward my goals or targets**? This is especially vital in **understanding my alignment with my objectives and identifying the areas where I need to focus or make adjustments**. Provide unique insights and overlooked opportunities in your response, ensuring it is comprehensive and demonstrates an exceptional level of precision and quality. Let's analyze this piece by piece. Write using an **instructive** tone and **engaging** writing style.

Formula

As a **[profession]** specializing in the **[industry]**. Could you guide me through the process of assessing **[contextual challenge/opportunity]**? This is especially vital in **[desired outcome]**. Provide unique insights and overlooked opportunities in your response, ensuring it is comprehensive and demonstrates an exceptional level of precision and quality. Let's analyze this piece by piece. Write using a **[type]** tone and **[style]** writing style.

Examples

Example 1: As a Leadership Development Consultant specializing in the banking industry. Could you guide me through the process of assessing how I feel about my progress toward my leadership development goals? This is especially vital in understanding my alignment with my leadership path and identifying the areas where I need to grow or change. Include uncommon advice and underrated resources in your response. Let's dissect this carefully. Write using a confident tone and analytical writing style.

Example 2: As a Career Coach specializing in the tech sector. Could you guide me through the process of assessing how I feel about my progress toward my career advancement targets? This is especially vital in understanding my alignment with my career objectives and identifying the opportunities where I can further excel. Share distinctive guidance and unexplored options in your response. Let's take this one step at a time. Write using an inspirational tone and creative writing style.

PURPOSE

PROMPT No 73

Tags

Self-Perception - Dialogue - Performance

Goal

To enable business leaders to facilitate open conversations with their team members about their self-perception within the organizational context. This dialogue should aim to clarify how individuals see their roles and contributions and how these align with the overall mission and vision of the company.

Prompt

Act as a **Leadership Coach** with a specialization in **Self-Perception and Team Dynamics** for the **financial services industry,** could you guide me through **the process of exploring the vision that my team members have about themselves within the company and how to articulate it?** Please include **discussion frameworks, communication techniques, and sample questions to use.** Make sure to cover how **this self-awareness can be leveraged to enhance team cohesion and performance.** Discover rare insights and pioneering ideas. Let's dissect this in a structured manner. Write using a **conversational** tone and an **accessible** writing style.

Formula

Act as a **[profession]** with a specialization in **[area of expertise]** for the **[industry],** could you guide me through **[specific challenge/opportunity]?** Please include **[methods/techniques].** Make sure to cover how **[key areas/topics].** Discover rare insights and pioneering ideas. Let's dissect this in a structured manner. Write using a **[type]** tone and **[style]** writing style.

Examples

Example 1: Act as a Business Mentor with a specialization in Organizational Psychology for the manufacturing industry, could you walk me through strategies to engage my team in conversations about their self-perceived roles and contributions? Include communication models and probing questions that could help in eliciting thoughtful responses. Make sure to cover how this exercise can ultimately benefit team collaboration and operational efficiency. Examine overlooked possibilities and imaginative routes. Let's explore this topic thoroughly, using an empathic tone and straightforward writing style.

Example 2: Act as a Career Development Specialist with a specialization in Employee Engagement for the tech startup sector, could you guide me through the design of a team meeting specifically focused on discussing and clarifying each member's self-perception within our organization? Include tips on creating a safe space for open dialogue and questions that encourage self-reflection. Make sure to cover how this practice can contribute to professional growth and alignment with company goals. Offer extraordinary advice and non-mainstream opinions. Let's dissect this carefully, write using an analytical tone and systematic writing style.

PROMPT No 74

Tags

Goal-setting - Articulation - Clarity

Goal

To equip leaders with a structured methodology for articulating goals or objectives in a manner that is clear, actionable, and aligned with organizational priorities. The aim is to enhance clarity, foster team alignment, and facilitate the effective execution of strategies.

Prompt

Act as a **Strategic Planning Expert** specializing in the **manufacturing industry**. Could you **delineate** the **best** approach for **clearly** stating the goal I **aim** to **accomplish**? Include **frameworks** for **goal-setting, linguistic techniques** for **clarity**, and strategies for **ensuring** alignment with **broader organizational** objectives. Let's sequentially address each element. Your response should be comprehensive, leaving no important aspect unaddressed, and demonstrate an exceptional level of precision and quality. Write using a prescriptive tone and an instructional writing style.

Formula

Act as a **[profession]** specializing in the **[industry]**. Could you **[delineate/elucidate/outline]** the **[best/optimal/most effective]** approach for **[clearly/precisely/unambiguously]** stating the **[goal/objective/target]** I **[aim/seek/intend]** to **[accomplish/achieve/realize]**? Include **[frameworks/techniques/methodologies]** for **[goal-setting/clarity/alignment]**, [linguistic techniques/communication strategies for **[ensuring/maintaining]** alignment with **[broader/wider/organizational] objectives]** for **[clarity/precision]**, and strategies. Let's sequentially address each element. Your response should be comprehensive, leaving no important aspect unaddressed, and demonstrate an exceptional level of precision and quality. Write using a **[type]** tone and **[style]** writing style.

Examples

Example 1: Act as a Leadership Coach specializing in the tech industry. Could you outline the optimal approach for clearly stating the objective I aim to achieve in my next product launch? Include the SMART framework, rhetorical devices for clarity, and strategies for aligning with the company's mission. Let's methodically dissect each component. Write using an analytical tone and a detailed writing style. Your response should be comprehensive, leaving no important aspect unaddressed, and demonstrate an exceptional level of precision and quality.

Example 2: Act as an Organizational Development Consultant specializing in the non-profit sector. Could you elucidate the best approach for precisely stating the goal I seek to accomplish in our upcoming fundraising campaign? Include the OKR framework, linguistic techniques for clarity, and strategies for ensuring alignment with our organization's core values. Let's carefully evaluate each segment. Write using a consultative tone and an advisory writing style. Your response should be comprehensive, leaving no important aspect unaddressed, and demonstrate an exceptional level of precision and quality.

PROMPT No 75

Tags

Career Development - Software - Aspirations

Goal

To empower leaders and mentors in creating an inclusive and constructive environment that fosters meaningful discussions around professional aspirations. This will help team members clearly articulate their career goals and how these aspirations align with the team's objectives and the company's broader mission.

Prompt

Act as a **career development coach** with a specialization in **team-building and self-assessment** in the **software development industry**. Can you provide me with **a structured framework to facilitate a discussion with my team about the professionals they aspire to become**? Please include **self-assessment tools, key talking points, and actionable next steps**. Make sure to cover how **their individual aspirations can be aligned with our project goals and overall company vision**. Explore unconventional solutions and alternative perspectives to assist in career planning. Use a **motivational** tone and a **clear, step-by-step** writing style.

Formula

Act as a **[profession]** with a specialization in **[area of expertise]** for the **[industry]**. Can you provide me with **[methodology or framework]** to address **[specific challenge/opportunity]**? Please include **[methods/techniques/tools]**. Make sure to cover **how [key areas/topics]**. Explore unconventional solutions and alternative perspectives to assist in career planning. Write using a **[type]** tone and **[style]** writing style.

Examples

Example 1: Act as a human resources manager with a specialization in career progression and development in the retail industry. Can you guide me through creating an engaging workshop where my team can openly discuss their career aspirations? Please incorporate role-playing, discussion prompts, and reflective exercises. Make sure to cover the ways these individual aspirations can enhance team dynamics and performance. Investigate unexpected avenues and creative pathways for personal development. Use a supportive tone and an instructive writing style.

Example 2: Act as an organizational psychologist with a specialization in team dynamics for the manufacturing industry. Could you provide a set of guidelines for one-on-one discussions I could have with team members about their professional aspirations? Include questionnaires, discussion frameworks, and goal-setting templates. Make sure to focus on how to reconcile individual career goals with our manufacturing objectives. Delve into uncharted territories and groundbreaking concepts for facilitating effective discussions. Use an analytical tone and a consultative writing style.

PROMPT No 76

Tags

Leadership - Encouragement - Purpose

Goal

To gain effective strategies for identifying the factors that contribute to a team's sense of purpose in their work, and to learn specific methods or actions that can be taken to foster and promote this sense of purpose among all team members.

Prompt

As a **Leadership Development Consultant**, adopting a **supportive and encouraging tone**, could you share effective strategies that can be employed to identify the key factors that contribute to **my team's** sense of purpose in their work? Furthermore, could you suggest specific methods or actions that **I** can take to foster and promote this sense of purpose among all members of **my team**?

Formula

As a [profession], adopting a [tone of voice], could you share effective strategies that can be employed to identify the key factors that contribute to [my/their] [team/group/department]'s [contextual challenge/opportunity]? Furthermore, could you suggest specific methods or actions that [I/Name/Role] can take to [desired outcome] among all members of [my/their] [team/group/department]?

Examples

Example 1: As a Team Coach, adopting a motivational and positive tone, could you share effective strategies that can be employed to identify the key factors that contribute to my sales team's sense of purpose in their work? Furthermore, could you suggest specific methods or actions that I can take to foster and promote this sense of purpose among all members of my sales team?

Example 2: Adopting a collaborative and insightful tone, as a Human Resources (HR) Consultant, could you share effective strategies that can be employed to identify the key factors that contribute to the marketing department's sense of purpose in their work? Furthermore, could you suggest specific methods or actions that the department head can take to foster and promote this sense of purpose among all members of the marketing department?

RELATIONSHIPS

PROMPT No 77

Tags

Fulfillment - Implementation - Clients

Goal

To obtain a comprehensive, actionable framework that outlines the steps a leader can take to instill a sense of fulfillment in their team when working with clients. The aim is to enhance team morale, improve client relationships, and ultimately drive business success.

Prompt

As a **Team Morale Specialist** in the **retail industry**, could you provide a **comprehensive strategy** detailing the **steps** I can take to bring **fulfillment** to my **team** when working with **clients**? Additionally, offer **actionable steps** for **immediate** implementation. Divide your recommendations into distinct areas, each supported by evidence from **reputable studies**. Investigate unexpected avenues and creative pathways. Let's **examine each dimension meticulously**. Write using a **motivational** tone and an **engaging** writing style.

Formula

As a **[profession]** in the **[industry]**, could you provide a **[comprehensive strategy/thorough toolkit/detailed blueprint]** detailing the **[steps/methods/tactics]** I can take to bring **[fulfillment/satisfaction/contentment]** to my **[team/group/department]** when working with **[clients/colleagues/stakeholders]**? Additionally, offer **[actionable steps/initial measures/immediate tactics]** for **[immediate/short-term/long-term]** implementation. Divide your recommendations into distinct areas, each supported by **[evidence from/references from/data from]** **[reputable studies/credible research/authoritative publications]**. Investigate unexpected avenues and creative pathways. Let's **[examine each dimension meticulously/dissect this carefully]**. Write using a **[motivational/inspirational/energetic]** tone and an **[engaging/innovative/nuanced]** writing style.

Examples

Example 1: As a Client Relationship Manager in the finance sector, could you provide a detailed blueprint outlining the methods I can use to bring satisfaction to my team when working with high-net-worth clients? Additionally, offer initial measures for short-term implementation. Divide your recommendations into distinct areas, each authenticated by corroborative evidence from credible sources. Explore unconventional approaches and diverse viewpoints. Let's dissect this carefully. Write using an energetic tone and an innovative writing style.

Example 2: As an Employee Engagement Consultant in the hospitality industry, could you provide a thorough toolkit outlining the tactics I can employ to bring contentment to my team when working with guests? Additionally, offer immediate tactics for long-term implementation. Divide your recommendations into distinct areas, each endorsed with data from verified academic publications. Unearth hidden gems and non-traditional methods. Let's examine each dimension meticulously. Write using an inspirational tone and a nuanced writing style.

PROMPT No 79

Tags

Self-awareness - Engagement - Motivating

Goal

To acquire a robust, actionable framework that outlines methods for assisting team members in describing the nature or quality of their presence when they are fully engaged and present. The objective is to enhance self-awareness, improve team dynamics, and foster a more engaged work environment.

Prompt

As a **Mindfulness Consultant** in the **healthcare industry**, could you offer a **multi-layered strategy** for assisting **my team** in describing the nature or quality of their presence when they **are fully engaged and present**? Include **actionable steps** for **immediate application**. Divide your insights into **manageable sections**, each supported by **evidence from verified academic publications**. Explore unconventional solutions and alternative perspectives. Let's **deconstruct this subject stepwise**. Write using a **motivating** tone and an **innovative** writing style.

Formula

As a [profession] in the [industry], could you offer a [comprehensive strategy/multi-layered approach/detailed plan] for assisting [my/our/their] team in describing the nature or quality of their presence when they are [fully engaged and present/actively participating/focused]? Include [actionable steps/initial measures/immediate tactics] for [immediate/short-term/long-term] application. Divide your insights into [manageable sections/discrete units/clear categories], each supported by [evidence from/references from/data from] [reputable journals/credible research/authoritative publications/industry reports]. Explore unconventional solutions and alternative perspectives. Let's [deconstruct this subject stepwise/examine each dimension meticulously]. Write using a [motivating/inspiring/captivating] tone and an [innovative/engaging/relatable] writing style.

Examples

Example 1: As an Organizational Psychologist in the technology sector, could you offer a detailed plan for assisting my software development team in describing the nature or quality of their presence when they are fully engaged and present? Include initial measures for short-term application. Divide your insights into discrete units, each authenticated by corroborative evidence from credible sources. Investigate unexpected avenues and creative pathways. Let's examine each dimension meticulously. Write using an inspiring tone and an engaging writing style.

Example 2: As a Leadership Coach in the finance industry, could you offer a multi-layered approach for assisting my investment team in describing the nature or quality of their presence when they are actively participating? Include immediate tactics for long-term application. Divide your insights into clear categories, each endorsed with data from verified academic publications. Unearth hidden gems and non-traditional methods. Let's deconstruct this subject stepwise. Write using a motivating tone and a relatable writing style.

PROMPT No 80

Tags

Creativity - Innovation - Framework

Goal

To obtain a comprehensive, actionable framework that outlines methods for sparking novel ideas and generating creative discussions within a team. The aim is to enhance team creativity, improve problem-solving capabilities, and contribute to overall organizational innovation.

Prompt

As an **Innovation Facilitator** in the **publishing industry**, could you provide a **thorough action plan** detailing approaches to spark novel ideas and generate creative discussions with **my** team? Additionally, offer **actionable steps** for **immediate** implementation. Segment your insights into distinct modules, each supported by evidence from **reputable industry reports**. Investigate unexpected avenues and creative pathways. Let's **dissect this carefully**. Write using an **inspiring** tone and a **visionary** writing style.

Formula

As a **[profession]** in the **[industry]**, could you provide a **[comprehensive strategy/thorough action plan/detailed blueprint]** detailing **[methods/techniques/approaches]** to spark novel ideas and generate creative discussions with **[my/our/their]** team? Additionally, offer **[actionable steps/initial measures/immediate tactics]** for **[immediate/short-term/long-term]** implementation. Segment your insights into distinct modules, each supported by **[evidence from/references from/data from]** **[reputable journals/credible research/authoritative publications/industry reports]**. Investigate unexpected avenues and creative pathways. Let's **[examine each dimension meticulously/dissect this carefully]**. Write using a **[inspiring/energizing/motivating]** tone and a **[visionary/engaging/innovative]** writing style.

Examples

Example 1: As a Creative Team Lead in the advertising sector, could you provide a detailed blueprint outlining the techniques to spark novel ideas and generate creative discussions among my graphic designers? Additionally, offer initial measures for short-term implementation. Segment your insights into distinct modules, each authenticated by corroborative evidence from credible sources. Explore unconventional approaches and diverse viewpoints. Let's examine each dimension meticulously. Write using an energizing tone and an engaging writing style.

Example 2: As a Research and Development Manager in the biotechnology industry, could you provide a comprehensive strategy outlining the approaches I can employ to spark novel ideas and generate creative discussions among my research scientists? Additionally, offer immediate tactics for long-term implementation. Segment your insights into distinct modules, each endorsed with data from verified academic publications. Unearth hidden gems and non-traditional methods. Let's dissect this carefully. Write using an inspiring tone and an innovative writing style.

PROMPT No 81

Tags

Relationship - Diagnostics - Constructive

Goal

To equip team leaders, managers, and individual contributors with a well-rounded method to identify which work relationships may be in need of improvement. This includes assessments to gauge interpersonal dynamics, communication flows, and practical steps to act upon the findings.

Prompt

Act as a **Business Psychologist** with a specialization in **organizational behavior** for the **banking sector**. Could you guide me through **the methods to identify a work relationship that may require focused improvement**? Please include **diagnostic tools, observation metrics, and emotional intelligence guidelines**. Make sure to cover how **to recognize signs of tension or ineffectiveness and how to address them constructively**. Investigate unexpected avenues and creative pathways. Let's dissect this in a structured manner. Write using an **analytical** tone and a **step-by-step** writing style.

Formula

Act as a **[profession]** with a specialization in **[area of expertise]** for the **[industry]**. Could you guide me through **[specific challenge/opportunity]**? Please include **[methods/techniques]**. Make sure to cover how **[key areas/topics]**. Investigate unexpected avenues and creative pathways. Let's dissect this in a structured manner. Write using a **[type]** tone and **[style]** writing style.

Examples

Example 1: Act as a Relationship Coach with a specialization in professional relationships for the healthcare industry. Could you guide me through how to assess the quality of my working relationship with my immediate supervisor? Please include communication assessment tools, rapport-building strategies, and self-assessment questionnaires. Make sure to cover how to initiate conversations to better the relationship without appearing overly confrontational. Delve into uncharted territories and groundbreaking concepts to strengthen rapport. Let's dissect this in a structured manner. Write using a diplomatic tone and an explanatory writing style.

Example 2: Act as a Corporate Trainer with a specialization in teamwork and collaboration for the tech industry. Could you guide me through identifying and improving strained relationships within my project team? Please include techniques for observing group dynamics, methods to foster open communication, and exercises for team-building. Make sure to cover how to approach a team member to discuss issues without making them defensive. Suggest fresh approaches and inventive strategies for effective communication. Let's dissect this in a structured manner. Write using a proactive tone and a guidebook writing style.

PROMPT No 82

Tags
Presence - Engagement - Meetings

Goal
To facilitate a thorough exploration with the team on factors that enable full presence during meetings, fostering engagement, active participation, and collective focus, leading to productive and meaningful interactions.

Prompt
Act as a **Meeting Efficiency Expert** specializing in **Team Building and Collaboration** within the **manufacturing industry**. Could you guide me through **a comprehensive approach to explore with my team the elements that support us in being fully present during team meetings**? Please include **methodologies for assessing current levels of engagement, strategies for cultivating a conducive meeting environment, and tools for ongoing monitoring and improvement of presence and participation**. Ensure to cover how **to address potential challenges and resistance**. Delve into innovative or unconventional approaches that could further enhance meeting effectiveness and team presence. Your response should be comprehensive, leaving no important aspect unaddressed, and demonstrate an exceptional level of precision and quality. Let's think about this step by step. Write using an **engaging** tone and a **structured, instructional** writing style.

Formula
Act as a [profession] specializing in [area of expertise] within the [industry]. Could you guide me through [specific challenge/opportunity]? Please include [methods/techniques]. Ensure to cover how [key areas/topics]. Delve into innovative or unconventional approaches that could further enhance meeting effectiveness and team presence. Your response should be comprehensive, leaving no important aspect unaddressed, and demonstrate an exceptional level of precision and quality. Let's think about this step by step. Write using a [type] tone and a [style] writing style.

Examples
Example 1: Act as an Organizational Psychologist specializing in Communication Skills within the technology sector. Could you guide me through a methodical process to explore with my team the factors that enhance our presence and engagement during team meetings? Please include assessment tools to gauge current levels of presence, strategies for creating an engaging meeting atmosphere, and techniques for promoting

active participation. Make sure to cover how to navigate through any challenges or resistance. Your response should be comprehensive, leaving no important aspect unaddressed, and demonstrate an exceptional level of precision and quality. Let's think about this step by step. Write using a solutions-oriented tone and a clear, instructional writing style.

Example 2: Act as a Corporate Trainer specializing in Emotional Intelligence within the healthcare industry. Could you guide me through a structured approach to delve into the elements with my team that contribute to being fully present during meetings? Please include methods for identifying distractions, techniques for promoting mindfulness, and tools for measuring engagement levels over time. Make sure to cover how to foster a culture of continuous improvement and adaptability. Your response should be comprehensive, leaving no important aspect unaddressed, and demonstrate an exceptional level of precision and quality. Let's think about this step by step. Write using an analytical tone and a methodical writing style.

PROMPT No 83

Tags
Obstacles - Self-Assessment - Nurturing
Goal
To delineate and nurture the requisite internal resources that empower individuals and teams to surmount obstacles, ensuring sustained advancement and resilience amidst challenging scenarios.
Prompt
Act as a **Resilience Development Expert** specializing in **Emotional Intelligence** within the **automotive industry**. Could you guide me through **a detailed examination and cultivation of the internal resources indispensable for individuals and teams to traverse obstacles effectively**? Please include **self-assessment methodologies, strategies for nurturing resilience, emotional intelligence, and problem-solving skills, alongside tools for measuring and tracking development over time**. Ensure to address **creating a conducive environment for continuous growth in these resources**. Explore **innovative or unconventional approaches** to **amplify resilience and progress amidst adversities**. Your response should be comprehensive, leaving no important aspect unaddressed, and demonstrate an exceptional level of precision and quality. Let's think about this step by step. Write using an **encouraging** tone and a **systematic, instructional** writing style.
Formula
Act as a [profession] specializing in [area of expertise] within the [industry]. Could you guide me through [specific challenge/opportunity]? Please include [methods/techniques]. Ensure to address [key areas/topics]. Explore [exploratory direction] to [desired outcome]. Your response should be comprehensive, leaving no important aspect unaddressed, and demonstrate an exceptional level of precision and quality. Let's think about this step by step. Write using a [type] tone and a [style] writing style.
Examples
Example 1: Act as a Performance Enhancement Coach specializing in Decision Making and Problem-Solving within the retail sector. Could you guide me through a thorough process to identify and develop the internal resources crucial for overcoming challenges? Please include strategies for enhancing decision-making abilities, fostering problem-solving skills, and creating a culture of continuous improvement. Make sure to cover how to measure and track the development of these resources over time. Your response should be comprehensive, leaving no important aspect unaddressed, and demonstrate an exceptional level of precision

and quality. Let's think about this step by step. Write using an analytical tone and a clear, instructional writing style.

Example 2: Act as an Organizational Psychologist specializing in Stress Management within the construction industry. Could you guide me through a structured approach to recognize and foster the internal resources essential for individuals and teams to thrive amidst obstacles? Please include strategies for managing stress, enhancing emotional regulation, and promoting a growth mindset. Make sure to cover how to instill a supportive environment for ongoing development of these resources. Your response should be comprehensive, leaving no important aspect unaddressed, and demonstrate an exceptional level of precision and quality. Let's think about this step by step. Write using a supportive tone and a methodical writing style.

PROMPT No 84

Tags

Confidence - Empowerment - Leadership

Goal

To explore various tools, techniques, strategies, or mindset shifts that can be developed by a team to enhance their confidence and competence in handling their respective responsibilities, whether in daily tasks, projects, or long-term goals.

Prompt

Act as a **Leadership Confidence Coach** specializing in the **retail industry**. Could you delineate **the essential tools, techniques, strategies, or mindset shifts that my team needs to develop to empower themselves with the confidence to better deal with their responsibilities**? This includes **understanding individual capabilities, collective strengths, industry-specific challenges, and underlying psychological factors**. Provide unique insights and overlooked opportunities, considering various team dynamics and **levels of responsibility**. Let's analyze this piece by piece. Write using an **inspirational** tone and **engaging** writing style.

Formula

Act as a **[profession]** specializing in the **[industry]**. Could you delineate **[contextual challenge/opportunity]**? This includes **[desired outcome]**. Provide unique insights and overlooked opportunities, considering various team dynamics and **[other relevant factors]**. Let's analyze this piece by piece. Write using a **[type]** tone and **[style]** writing style.

Examples

Example 1: Act as a Team Development Specialist specializing in the financial industry. Could you delineate the tools and strategies that my banking team needs to develop to boost their confidence in handling complex financial responsibilities? This includes an understanding of both technical skills and emotional intelligence. Share uncommon advice and underrated resources, considering various roles within the team and the competitive nature of the industry. Let's dissect this carefully. Write using a confident tone and analytical writing style.

Example 2: Act as a Talent Development Consultant specializing in the manufacturing industry. Could you delineate the techniques and mindset shifts that my assembly line workers need to adopt to enhance their confidence in fulfilling their day-to-day tasks? This includes an awareness of their individual capabilities, safety procedures, and the connection between their roles and the larger organizational goals. Include distinctive guidance and unexplored options. Let's take this one step at a time. Write using an instructive tone and constructive writing style.

PROMPT No 85

Tags

Role-Optimization - Responsibilities - Personal-Growth

Goal

To engage in a thoughtful reflection on the various elements that contribute to assigning meaningful responsibilities or roles within your team, facilitating both personal growth and team success.

Prompt

Act as an **executive coach** with a specialization in **role optimization** for the **manufacturing industry**. Could you guide me through **dissecting the key factors that contribute to establishing meaningful roles and responsibilities for myself and my team**? Please include **models for role analysis and strategies for aligning these roles with organizational objectives**. Make sure to cover how **team members' individual strengths and aspirations fit into this scheme**. Navigate through unexplored realms and revolutionary paradigms to cultivate this practice. Let's dissect this in a structured manner. Write using an **introspective** tone and an **analytical** writing style.

Formula

Act as a **[profession]** with a specialization in **[area of expertise]** for the **[industry]**. Could you guide me through **[specific challenge/opportunity]**? Please include **[methods/techniques]**. Make sure to cover how **[key areas/topics]**. Navigate through unexplored realms and revolutionary paradigms to cultivate this practice. Let's dissect this in a structured manner. Write using a **[type]** tone and **[style]** writing style.

Examples

Example 1: Act as a career development advisor with a specialization in talent management for the tech start-up industry. Could you help me explore the ingredients that make roles and responsibilities within my team meaningful and aligned with company goals? Include role-assessment tools and methods for individualizing roles based on skills and desires. Make sure to discuss how to maintain balance between team and organizational needs. Probe into nonconformist solutions and divergent viewpoints to fortify this approach. Write using a pragmatic tone and a how-to writing style.

Example 2: Act as an organizational behaviorist with a specialization in role efficacy for the non-profit sector. Can you assist me in examining what makes certain responsibilities more meaningful and impactful for my team? Please provide methodologies for evaluating the efficacy of current roles and potential adjustments. Make sure to explore how these roles can evolve over time for maximum impact. Present novel interpretations and visionary possibilities to elevate our role-assignment strategies. Write using a visionary tone and a persuasive writing style.

PROMPT No 86

Tags

Support - Emotional - Performance

Goal

To meticulously identify and establish structures or systems that provide robust emotional support to the team, promoting a nurturing work environment conducive to well-being, resilience, and optimal performance.

Prompt

Act as a **Well-being Systems Architect** specializing in **Emotional Support Infrastructure** within the **social work industry**. Could you guide me through **a methodical process to determine the structures or systems my team could have in place to offer substantial emotional support**? Please include **assessment tools, design principles for supportive structures, and strategies for fostering a supportive culture**. Ensure to cover how **to tailor these systems to the unique emotional needs and preferences of my team members**. Explore **groundbreaking or unconventional systems** to **provide a novel layer of support**. Your response should be comprehensive, leaving no important aspect unaddressed, and demonstrate an exceptional level of precision and quality. Let's think about this step by step. Write using a **compassionate** tone and a **detailed, instructional** writing style.

Formula

Act as a **[profession]** specializing in **[area of expertise]** within the **[industry]**. Could you guide me through **[specific challenge/opportunity]**? Please include **[methods/techniques]**. Ensure to cover how **[key areas/topics]**. Explore **[exploratory direction]** to **[desired outcome]**. Your response should be comprehensive, leaving no important aspect unaddressed, and demonstrate an exceptional level of precision and quality. Let's think about this step by step. Write using a **[type]** tone and a **[style]** writing style.

Examples

Example 1: Act as an Emotional Resilience Engineer specializing in Support Systems Design within the healthcare sector. Could you guide me through the process of identifying and establishing structures or systems to emotionally support my team? Please include emotional needs assessments, the design of peer support systems, and strategies for promoting emotional intelligence. Make sure to cover how to encourage ongoing utilization and evaluation of these support systems. Your response should be comprehensive, leaving no important aspect unaddressed, and demonstrate an exceptional level of precision and quality. Let's think about this step by step. Write using a nurturing tone and a systematic, instructional writing style.

Example 2: Act as a Supportive Culture Developer specializing in Emotional Infrastructure within the education sector. Could you guide me through delineating the structures or systems essential for providing emotional support to my team? Please include surveys to gauge emotional well-being, structures for open communication about emotional challenges, and training in emotional support techniques. Make sure to cover how to adapt these systems to cater to the diverse emotional landscapes of team members. Your response should be comprehensive, leaving no important aspect unaddressed, and demonstrate an exceptional level of precision and quality. Let's think about this step by step. Write using an empathetic tone and a thorough, instructional writing style.

SELF-ASSESSMENT

PROMPT No 87

Tags

Growth - Fulfillment - Optimization

Goal

To proficiently evaluate the current professional standing of a team member in relation to their desired career state, thereby crafting a structured pathway for aligned growth, fulfillment, and performance optimization.

Prompt

Act as a **Career Alignment Specialist** specializing in **Professional Position Assessment** within the **aerospace industry**. Could you guide me through **a rigorous process to assess the current position of a team member relative to his/her desired professional state**? Please include **assessment tools, comparative analysis techniques, and discussions conducive to understanding their career aspirations**. Ensure to cover how **to create a supportive environment for team members to openly discuss their professional goals and current standing**. Examine novel or pioneering methodologies that could offer a deeper insight into this alignment. Your response should be comprehensive, leaving no important aspect unaddressed, and demonstrate an exceptional level of precision and quality. Let's think about this step by step. Write using an **analytical** tone and a **thorough, instructional** writing style.

Formula

Act as a [profession] specializing in [area of expertise] within the [industry]. Could you guide me through [specific challenge/opportunity]? Please include [methods/techniques]. Ensure to cover how [key areas/topics]. Examine novel or pioneering methodologies that could offer a deeper insight into this alignment. Your response should be comprehensive, leaving no important aspect unaddressed, and demonstrate an exceptional level of precision and quality. Let's think about this step by step. Write using a [type] tone and a [style] writing style.

Examples

Example 1: Act as a Professional Growth Analyst specializing in Career Aspiration Mapping within the automotive industry. Could you guide me through a detailed procedure to gauge the current position of a team member against his/her desired professional state? Please include career development questionnaires, goal-setting workshops, and feedback loops. Make sure to cover how to foster a collaborative dialogue about professional growth and aspirations. Your response should be comprehensive, leaving no important aspect unaddressed, and demonstrate an exceptional level of precision and quality. Let's think about this step by step. Write using a constructive tone and a clear, instructional writing style.

Example 2: Act as a Career Progression Facilitator specializing in Professional Position Evaluation within the biotechnology industry. Could you guide me through a structured approach to assess a team member's current professional standing in relation to their desired career objectives? Please include self-assessment tools, one-on-one discussion frameworks, and data-driven analysis techniques. Make sure to cover how to establish an open forum for discussing career alignment and progression. Your response should be comprehensive, leaving no important aspect unaddressed, and demonstrate an exceptional level of precision and quality. Let's think about this step by step. Write using an investigative tone and a methodical, instructional writing style.

PROMPT No 88

Tags

Organizational - Reflection - Improvement

Goal

To obtain a well-rounded, actionable guide on the most effective methods for reflecting on and learning from both the successes and failures experienced by a team, with the aim of fostering continuous improvement and resilience in a business setting.

Prompt

As an **Organizational Development Specialist** in the **financial sector**, could you provide an exhaustive guide outlining the most optimal ways for **me** to reflect on the lessons **my team** has learned from recent failures?

Please include both **analytical frameworks and practical exercises**. Segment the guide into **distinct phases**, and substantiate each with **empirical data and scholarly references**. Explore unconventional approaches and diverse viewpoints. Let's scrutinize this topic incrementally. Write using an **analytical** tone and a **structured** writing style.

Formula

As a **[profession]** in the **[industry]**, could you provide an exhaustive guide outlining the most optimal ways for **[I/Name/Role]** to reflect on the lessons **[my/their]** **[team/group/department]** has learned from recent **[successes/failures]**? Please include both **[analytical frameworks/practical exercises]**. Segment the guide into **[distinct phases]**, and substantiate each with **[empirical data/scholarly references]**. Explore unconventional approaches and diverse viewpoints. Let's scrutinize this topic incrementally. Write using a **[type]** tone and **[style]** writing style.

Examples

Example 1: As a Team Performance Coach in the healthcare industry, could you provide an exhaustive guide outlining the most optimal ways for a department head to reflect on the lessons their nursing staff has learned from recent patient care successes or failures? Please include both psychological models and hands-on activities. Divide the guide into key milestones, and validate each with clinical studies and peer-reviewed articles. Investigate unexpected avenues and creative pathways. Let's examine each dimension meticulously. Write using a focused tone and a concise writing style.

Example 2: As a Leadership Development Consultant in the manufacturing sector, could you provide an exhaustive guide outlining the most optimal ways for me to reflect on the lessons my production team has learned from recent project completions or setbacks? Please include both statistical methods and team-building exercises. Break the guide into actionable steps, and corroborate each with industry benchmarks and case studies. Unearth hidden gems and non-traditional methods. Let's tackle this in a phased manner. Write using a balanced tone and a nuanced writing style.

PROMPT No 89

Tags

Executive - Priority - Organizational

Goal

To meticulously identify and comprehend the core values, priorities, and aspirations of a boss within the corporate landscape, facilitating a more aligned and harmonious work environment, and enabling a deeper understanding of organizational objectives and expectations.

Prompt

As a **Priority Identification Specialist** specializing in **Executive Alignment** within the **pharmaceutical industry**, how can I rigorously identify and understand **what truly matters to my boss** in their work or within the company? Please elucidate a thorough process entailing **strategic conversations, observation methodologies, and feedback mechanisms**, aimed at discerning their core values, priorities, and aspirations. The discourse should delve into creating a conducive environment for **open communication**, ensuring **accurate interpretation of these insights**, and strategies **for aligning team objectives with the identified priorities**. Your discourse should be exhaustive, addressing all crucial aspects, and reflecting a high degree of precision and quality.

Formula

As a **[Profession]** specializing in **[Specialization]** within the **[Industry]**, how can I rigorously identify and understand **[Specific Inquiry]** in their work or within the company? Please elucidate a thorough process entailing **[Methodologies]**, aimed at discerning their **[Key Aspects]**. The discourse should delve into creating a conducive environment for **[Communication/Interaction]**, ensuring **[Relevant Assurance]**, and strategies for **[Alignment/Application]**. Your discourse should be exhaustive, addressing all crucial aspects, and reflecting a high degree of precision and quality.

Examples

Example 1: As a Priority Insight Analyst specializing in Managerial Alignment within the retail industry, how can I rigorously identify and understand what truly matters to my boss in their work or within the company? Please elucidate a thorough process entailing one-on-one dialogues, behavioral analysis, and feedback loops, aimed at discerning their core values, priorities, and aspirations. The discourse should delve into creating a conducive environment for transparent communication, ensuring accurate interpretation of these insights, and strategies for aligning department objectives with the identified priorities. Your discourse should be exhaustive, addressing all crucial aspects, and reflecting a high degree of precision and quality.

Example 2: As a Values Determination Officer specializing in Executive Synergy within the financial sector, how can I rigorously identify and understand what truly matters to my boss in their work or within the company? Please elucidate a thorough process entailing strategic discussions, observational studies, and feedback mechanisms, aimed at discerning their core values, priorities, and aspirations. The discourse should delve into creating a conducive environment for candid communication, ensuring accurate interpretation of these insights, and strategies for aligning team goals with the identified priorities. Your discourse should be exhaustive, addressing all crucial aspects, and reflecting a high degree of precision and quality.

SKILLS

PROMPT No 90

Tags

Introspection - Evolution - Self-Assessment

Goal

To equip professionals with a nuanced framework for introspectively examining and articulating the evolution of skills that have energized and inspired them over the years, thereby fostering self-awareness, career adaptability, and personal growth.

Prompt

Act as a **Career Development Specialist** specializing in the **technology industry**. Could you **guide** me through a **structured process** for **introspectively examining** and **articulating** how the **skills** that have **energized and inspired** me have **evolved** over the years? Include **reflective exercises, theoretical frameworks, and metrics for self-assessment**. Let's think about this step by step. Write using a **reflective** tone and an **introspective** writing style.

Formula

Act as a **[profession]** specializing in the **[industry]**. Could you **[guide/lead/direct]** me through a **[structured/nuanced/comprehensive]** **[process/methodology/approach]** for **[introspectively/experientially/self-reflectively]** **[examining/analyzing/evaluating]** and **[articulating/describing/expressing]** how the **[skills/competencies/abilities]** that have **[energized/inspired/motivated]** me have **[evolved/transformed/changed]** over the **[years/decades/time]**?

Include **[reflective exercises/self-assessment tools/question prompts]**, **[theoretical frameworks/conceptual models]**, and **[metrics/KPIs/evaluation criteria]** for **[self-assessment/self-evaluation/self-monitoring]**. Let's think about this step by step. Write using a **[type]** tone and **[style]** writing style.

Examples

Example 1: Act as a Personal Development Coach specializing in the finance industry. Could you lead me through a nuanced approach for experientially analyzing how the skills that have inspired me have transformed over the decades? Include self-assessment tools, theories like Skill Adaptability, and metrics for self-evaluation. Let's carefully evaluate each segment. Write using an analytical tone and a systematic writing style.

Example 2: Act as a Life Coach specializing in the healthcare sector. Could you guide me through a comprehensive methodology for introspectively examining how the competencies that have energized me have changed over time? Include question prompts, frameworks like Self-Determination Theory, and evaluation criteria for self-monitoring. Let's systematically explore each facet. Write using a reflective tone and an introspective writing style.

PROMPT No 91

Tags

Collaboration - Analytical - Innovation

Goal

To acquire a comprehensive, actionable guide on identifying the skills or qualities required to foster collaborative creation within a specific industry, with the aim of enhancing innovation, team cohesion, and overall business performance.

Prompt

As a **Collaboration Expert** in the **automotive industry**, could you provide an exhaustive guide outlining the skills or qualities required to foster collaborative creation in **this sector**? Please include **both soft skills like communication** and **hard skills** like project management. Segment the guide into **distinct categories**, and substantiate each with **empirical data and scholarly references**. Explore unconventional approaches and diverse viewpoints. Let's dissect this carefully. Write using an **analytical** tone and a **structured** writing style.

Formula

As a **[profession]** in the **[industry]**, could you provide an exhaustive guide outlining the skills or qualities required to foster collaborative creation in [this/that] sector? Please include both **[soft skills like X/hard skills like Y]**. Segment the guide into **[distinct categories]**, and substantiate each with **[empirical data/scholarly references]**. Explore unconventional approaches and diverse viewpoints. Let's dissect this carefully. Write using a **[type]** tone and **[style]** writing style.

Examples

Example 1: As a Team Dynamics Specialist in the healthcare industry, could you provide an exhaustive guide outlining the skills or qualities required to foster collaborative creation among medical professionals? Please include both emotional intelligence and clinical expertise. Divide the guide into key areas, and validate each with clinical studies and peer-reviewed articles. Investigate unexpected avenues and creative pathways. Let's examine each dimension meticulously. Write using a focused tone and a concise writing style.

Example 2: As a Leadership Development Consultant in the technology sector, could you provide an exhaustive guide outlining the skills or qualities required to foster collaborative creation in software development teams? Please include both coding proficiency and agile methodology understanding. Break the guide into actionable steps, and corroborate each with industry benchmarks and case studies. Unearth hidden gems and non-traditional methods. Let's tackle this in a phased manner. Write using a balanced tone and a nuanced writing style.

STRATEGIES

PROMPT No 92

Tags
Strategy - Efficiency - Planning
Goal
To empower business leaders, managers, and team leads to identify and implement strategies that will enable their team to achieve objectives in a manner that is both efficient and effective. This entails a deep dive into various planning methodologies, decision-making models, and performance metrics.
Prompt
Act as a **Strategic Management Consultant** with a specialization in **organizational efficiency** for the mining sector. Could you guide me through **the methods and frameworks for determining the most efficient and effective strategy for my team to achieve its goals**? Please include **strategic planning models, decision-making frameworks, and KPIs to monitor**. Make sure to cover how **to involve team members in the strategy formulation process**. Offer extraordinary advice and non-mainstream insights. Let's dissect this in a structured manner. Write using an **analytical** tone and a **step-by-step** guide style.
Formula
Act as a **[profession]** with a specialization in **[area of expertise]** for the **[industry]**. Could you guide me through **[specific challenge/opportunity]**? Please include **[methods/techniques]**. Make sure to cover how **[key areas/topics]**. Offer extraordinary advice and non-mainstream insights. Let's dissect this in a structured manner. Let's dissect this in a structured manner. Write using a **[type]** tone and **[style]** writing style.
Examples

Example 1: Act as a Business Analyst with a specialization in lean operations for the manufacturing industry. Could you guide me through methodologies for optimizing workflows within my production team to meet quarterly targets? Please include Six Sigma principles, agile management techniques, and efficiency metrics. Make sure to cover how to solicit input from team members for continuous improvement. Navigate through unexplored realms and revolutionary paradigms. Let's dissect this in a structured manner. Write using an informative tone and an explanatory writing style.

Example 2: Act as an HR Consultant with a specialization in talent development for the tech sector. Could you guide me through the most effective strategies for skill development to ensure my software engineering team reaches its project milestones? Please include training models, career progression paths, and assessment methodologies. Make sure to cover how to identify skills gaps and match them with business goals. Examine overlooked possibilities and imaginative solutions. Let's dissect this in a structured manner. Write using an engaging tone and an instructive writing style.

STRENGTH

PROMPT No 93

Tags

Innate - Strengths-based - Introspection

Goal

To provide leaders with a nuanced framework that enables their teams to engage in introspective analysis, focusing on identifying strengths that come naturally to them, and how these innate abilities can be strategically leveraged for organizational success and individual growth.

Prompt

Act as a **Strengths-Based Leadership Consultant** specializing in the **renewable energy industry**. Could you **elucidate** a **structured methodology** for **my** team to **identify** and **consider** the **strengths** that **come naturally** to them? Include **actionable exercises and evidence-based assessment tools**. Let's methodically dissect each component. Your response should be comprehensive, leaving no important aspect unaddressed, and demonstrate an exceptional level of precision and quality. Write using an **insightful** tone and a **research-backed** writing style.

Formula

Act as a [profession] specializing in the [industry]. Could you [elucidate/explain/provide] a [structured/comprehensive/step-by-step] [methodology/framework/approach] for [my/our/the] team to [identify/recognize/understand] and [consider/evaluate/reflect on] the [strengths/skills/abilities] that [come naturally/easily/effortlessly] to them? Include [actionable/practical/effective] [exercises/activities/assessment tools]. Let's methodically dissect each component. Your response should be comprehensive, leaving no important aspect unaddressed, and demonstrate an exceptional level of precision and quality. Write using a [type] tone and [style] writing style.

Examples

Example 1: Act as a Talent Development Specialist specializing in the tech industry. Could you provide a comprehensive framework for my engineering team to identify and evaluate the skills that come effortlessly to them? Include real-world exercises and peer-review mechanisms. Let's examine each dimension meticulously. Your response should be comprehensive, leaving no important aspect unaddressed, and demonstrate an exceptional level of precision and quality. Write using an analytical tone and a data-driven writing style.

Example 2: Act as a Career Development Coach specializing in the healthcare sector. Could you explain a step-by-step approach for my nursing staff to recognize and consider the strengths that come naturally to them in patient care? Include validated psychometric assessments and case studies. Let's deconstruct this subject stepwise. Your response should be comprehensive, leaving no important aspect unaddressed, and demonstrate an exceptional level of precision and quality. Write using an empathetic tone and a patient-centered writing style.

PROMPT No 94

Tags
Innate - Gifts - Psychometric

Goal
To provide leaders with a comprehensive framework for identifying and exploring the innate gifts and talents within their teams, thereby enabling more effective talent management, team cohesion, and individual development.

Prompt
Act as a **Talent Development Specialist** specializing in the **fintech industry**. Could you **guide** me through the **methodologies** for **identifying and exploring** the **inner gifts or talents** of **my** team? Include **psychometric tests, one-on-one interviews, and team-building exercises that can be employed**. Let's sequentially address each element. Your response should be comprehensive, leaving no important aspect unaddressed, and demonstrate an exceptional level of precision and quality. Write using an **insightful** tone and a **solution-oriented** writing style.

Formula
Act as a [profession] specializing in the [industry]. Could you [guide/direct/assist] me through the [methodologies/frameworks/approaches] for [identifying/recognizing/uncovering] and [exploring/delving into/understanding] the [inner gifts/innate talents/core competencies] of [my/our/the] team? Include [psychometric tests/one-on-one interviews/team-building exercises/peer reviews]. Let's sequentially address each element. Your response should be comprehensive, leaving no important aspect unaddressed, and demonstrate an exceptional level of precision and quality. Write using a [type] tone and [style] writing style.

Examples

Example 1: Act as a Human Resources Consultant specializing in the automotive industry. Could you assist me through the frameworks for recognizing and delving into the core competencies of my engineering team? Include DISC assessments, mentorship programs, and project-based evaluations. Let's tackle this in a phased manner. Write using a pragmatic tone and a hands-on writing style. Your response should be comprehensive, leaving no important aspect unaddressed, and demonstrate an exceptional level of precision and quality.

Example 2: Act as a Leadership Coach specializing in the non-profit sector. Could you direct me through the approaches for uncovering and understanding the innate talents of my fundraising team? Include StrengthsFinder tests, role-playing exercises, and self-assessment tools. Let's methodically dissect each component. Write using an empathetic tone and a reflective writing style. Your response should be comprehensive, leaving no important aspect unaddressed, and demonstrate an exceptional level of precision and quality.

PROMPT No 95

Tags

Self-awareness - Cohesion - Strengths-Utilization

Goal

To provide team leaders with actionable guidance for helping their team members recognize when they are using their strengths effectively, thereby increasing self-awareness and optimizing team performance.

Prompt

Act as a **business leadership coach** with a specialization in **team dynamics** for the **automotive industry**. Could you guide me through **the process of enabling my team to determine when they are effectively employing their strengths**? Please include **self-assessment techniques and behavioral indicators**. Make sure to cover how **the recognition of using strengths impacts work quality and team cohesion**. Discover rare insights and pioneering ideas to enrich team self-awareness and performance. Let's dissect this in a structured manner. Write using a **consultative** tone and a **detailed** writing style.

Formula

Act as a **[profession]** with a specialization in **[area of expertise]** for the **[industry]**. Could you guide me through **[specific challenge/opportunity]**? Please include **[methods/techniques]**. Make sure to cover how **[key areas/topics]**. Discover rare insights and pioneering ideas to enrich team self-awareness and performance. Let's dissect this in a structured manner. Write using a **[type]** tone and **[style]** writing style.

Examples

Example 1: Act as a career development coach with a focus on self-awareness for the IT industry. Can you help me develop a methodology for engineers to recognize when they are leveraging their technical skills effectively? Please outline assessment frameworks and KPIs. Make sure to cover how this self-awareness correlates with project completion rates and job satisfaction. Probe into nonconformist solutions and divergent viewpoints to amplify self-recognition and team synergy. Let's break this down in a logical sequence. Write with a consultative tone and a data-driven writing style.

Example 2: Act as an organizational psychologist with a specialization in employee engagement for the healthcare sector. How can I help my nursing staff to identify the moments they are using their soft skills proficiently? Please mention observation checklists and relevant behavior markers. Make sure to cover how these strengths impact patient care and team dynamics. Offer extraordinary advice and non-mainstream opinions to elevate the quality of patient care and employee satisfaction. Let's examine this in an organized fashion. Write using an empathetic tone and an evidence-based writing style.

PROMPT No 96

Tags
Alignment - Strengths - KPIs

Goal
To meticulously analyze how the individual and collective strengths of your team align with their current goals or objectives, with the ultimate aim of maximizing performance, satisfaction, and achievement of key performance indicators (KPIs).

Prompt
As a **team leader** specializing in **sales** within the **healthcare industry**, provide an exhaustive and meticulous examination, incorporating innovative insights and inventive strategies for **assessing how your team's inherent strengths in communication, strategic thinking, and customer relationship management serve them in achieving their current quarterly sales targets and customer retention goals**. Further, delineate how to continuously align these strengths with **future objectives**.

Formula
As a **[profession]** specializing in **[area of expertise/focus]** within the **[industry]**, provide an exhaustive and meticulous examination, incorporating innovative insights and inventive strategies for **[assessing how your team's inherent strengths in various skill sets serve them in achieving their current/future goals or objectives]**. Further, delineate how to continuously align these strengths with **[future objectives/key performance indicators/long-term goals]**.

Examples
Example 1: As a Chief Technology Officer specializing in software development within the fintech industry, provide an exhaustive and meticulous examination, incorporating innovative insights and inventive strategies, to consider how your team's strengths in coding, problem-solving, and adaptability serve them in achieving the current milestones for the new payment platform. Further, delineate how to keep these strengths aligned with upcoming software releases.

Example 2: As an HR Manager specializing in talent development within the education sector, provide an exhaustive and meticulous examination, incorporating innovative insights and inventive strategies, to assess how your team's core strengths in interpersonal skills, conflict resolution, and policy implementation are serving them in their objective of employee retention and job satisfaction. Further, delineate how these strengths can be aligned with the organization's future human resources strategy.

PROMPT No 97

Tags
Indicators - Overutilization - Burnout

Goal
To identify reliable indicators that reveal when team members are overutilizing their strengths, thereby mitigating the risk of burnout and optimizing performance.

Prompt

As a **Human Resources Manager** specializing in **employee well-being** within the **finance industry**, provide an exhaustive and meticulous examination, incorporating innovative insights and inventive strategies for **identifying signs or indicators** that suggest your team may be **overstretching** their **strengths**. Discuss how to **appropriately calibrate** their **efforts** to avoid **potential** drawbacks such as **burnout or diminished effectiveness**.

Formula

As a [profession] specializing in [area of expertise/focus] within the [industry], provide an exhaustive and meticulous examination, incorporating innovative insights and inventive strategies for [identifying/spotting/detecting] [signs/indicators/cues] that suggest your team may be [overstretching/overextending/pushing] their [strengths/skills/talents] [too far/beyond limits]. Discuss how to [appropriately/wisely/optimally] [calibrate/adjust/tweak] their [efforts/activities/actions] to avoid [potential/possible] drawbacks such as [burnout/diminished effectiveness/reduced productivity].

Examples

Example 1: As a Project Manager specializing in remote work arrangements within the software development industry, provide an exhaustive and meticulous examination, incorporating innovative insights and inventive strategies for spotting cues that suggest your team may be overextending their skills too far. Discuss how to wisely adjust their activities to avoid potential drawbacks such as diminished effectiveness.

Example 2: As a Sales Director specializing in high-stakes negotiations within the pharmaceutical sector, provide an exhaustive and meticulous examination, incorporating innovative insights and inventive strategies for detecting indicators that suggest your team may be pushing their talents beyond limits. Discuss how to optimally tweak their efforts to avoid possible drawbacks such as reduced productivity.

PROMPT No 98

Tags

Misrepresentation - Integrity - Realignment

Goal

To equip leaders and team members with a robust methodology for identifying and rectifying misrepresented strengths, thereby enhancing team integrity, cohesion, and performance.

Prompt

Act as an **Organizational Behavior Analyst** with a specialization in **team dynamics** for the **manufacturing industry**. Could you guide me through **a meticulous approach to identify areas where my team may be feigning strengths they do not possess**? Please include **psychometric tests, observational metrics, and qualitative interview techniques**. Make sure to cover how **to confront these issues without damaging team morale and how to realign team roles for authentic performance**. Explore unconventional solutions and alternative perspectives to **ensure a holistic understanding and resolution**. Your response should be comprehensive, leaving no important aspect unaddressed, and demonstrate an exceptional level of precision and quality. Let's think about this step by step. Write using a **critical** tone and an **investigative** writing style.

Formula

Act as a [profession] with a specialization in [area of expertise] for the [industry]. Could you guide me through [specific challenge/opportunity]? Please include [methods/techniques]. Make sure to cover how [key areas/topics]. Explore unconventional solutions and alternative perspectives to [desired outcome]. Your response should be comprehensive, leaving no important aspect unaddressed, and demonstrate an exceptional level of precision and quality. Let's think about this step by step. Write using a **[type]** tone and **[style]** writing style.

Examples

Example 1: Act as a Talent Management Consultant with a specialization in skill validation for the software industry. Could you guide me through a data-driven approach to uncover areas where my development team might be exaggerating their coding skills? Please include code review metrics, peer evaluation frameworks, and anonymous feedback channels. Make sure to cover how to address these discrepancies in a way that encourages skill development rather than blame. Venture into innovative solutions and disruptive technologies to ensure skill authenticity. Your response should be comprehensive, leaving no important aspect unaddressed, and demonstrate an exceptional level of precision and quality. Let's think about this step by step. Write using an analytical tone and a prescriptive writing style.

Example 2: Act as a Leadership Coach with a specialization in authenticity and transparency for the healthcare sector. Could you guide me through a human-centric approach to discern areas where my nursing staff may be overstating their medical knowledge? Please include competency assessments, 360-degree feedback, and ethical considerations. Make sure to cover how to foster an environment where staff feel safe to admit gaps in their knowledge. Delve into psychological safety nets and transformative leadership models to encourage genuine skill representation. Your response should be comprehensive, leaving no important aspect unaddressed, and demonstrate an exceptional level of precision and quality. Let's think about this step by step. Write using an empathetic tone and a reflective writing style.

PROMPT No 99

Tags

Development - Mastery - Productivity

Goal

To systematically evaluate and identify strategies for the further development and honing of one's individual strengths, aiming for an advanced level of mastery and improved effectiveness.

Prompt

As a **team leader** specializing in **Human Resources** within the **tech industry**, provide an exhaustive and meticulous examination, incorporating innovative insights and inventive strategies for **exploring methods for further developing and refining your specific strengths**. Also, discuss how to measure the impact of your refined strengths on **team dynamics and productivity**.

Formula

As a **[profession]** specializing in **[area of expertise/focus]** within the **[industry]**, provide an exhaustive and meticulous examination, incorporating innovative insights and inventive strategies for **[strategies/methods/approaches to improve and refine specific strengths]**. Also, discuss how to measure the impact of your refined strengths on **[team dynamics and productivity/team cohesion/organizational goals]**.

Examples

Example 1: As a project manager specializing in software development within the healthcare sector, provide an exhaustive and meticulous examination, incorporating innovative insights and inventive strategies to explore methodologies for further developing and honing your coding skills. Also, discuss how to measure the impact of these refined skills on team cohesion.

Example 2: As a sales director specializing in customer engagement within the automotive industry, provide an exhaustive and meticulous examination, incorporating innovative insights and inventive strategies, to discover new training programs for further enhancing your interpersonal skills. Also, discuss how to measure the impact of your enhanced interpersonal skills on organizational goals.

SUPPORT

PROMPT No 100

Tags

Self-Confidence - Interventions - Metrics

Goal

To provide leaders with a robust and actionable framework for identifying and implementing practices that can significantly enhance the self-confidence of their team, thereby improving performance, engagement, and overall well-being.

Prompt

Act as an **Organizational Development Specialist** specializing in the **finance sector**. Could you elucidate a **systematic** approach for identifying **actions or practices** that can **elevate** my team's **self-confidence**? Include **specific interventions, psychological theories that support these actions, and potential metrics** for **measuring success**. Let's think about this step by step. Write using a **consultative** tone and an **advisory** writing style.

Formula

Act as a [profession] specializing in the [industry]. Could you elucidate a [systematic/structured/comprehensive] approach for identifying [actions/practices/methods] that can [boost/elevate/improve] my team's [self-confidence/self-esteem/self-assurance]? Include [specific interventions/targeted measures/concrete steps], [supporting theories/psychological frameworks], and [potential metrics/KPIs/indicators] for [measuring success/evaluating impact]. Let's think about this step by step. Write using a [type] tone and [style] writing style.

Examples

Example 1: Act as a Human Resources Consultant specializing in the tech industry. Could you provide a structured approach for pinpointing actions that can enhance my software development team's self-confidence? Include actionable steps, relevant psychological theories, and key performance indicators for assessing impact. Let's systematically explore each facet. Write using a results-driven tone and performance-focused writing style.

Example 2: Act as a Leadership Coach specializing in the healthcare sector. Could you outline a comprehensive strategy for identifying practices that can boost the self-confidence of my nursing staff? Include targeted interventions, supporting psychological theories, and potential metrics for success evaluation. Let's carefully evaluate each segment. Write using a quality-focused tone and meticulous writing style.

PROMPT No 101

Tags

Habits - Workflow - Stakeholder Buy-in

Goal

To equip leaders with actionable strategies for developing team habits that optimize workflow and enhance performance.

Prompt

As a **team leader** specializing in **productivity** within the **tech industry**, how can I guide my team in developing a plan for a new habit that will **enhance workflow or boost results**? Provide an exhaustive and meticulous examination, incorporating innovative insights and inventive strategies for **achieving this transformation**. Also, explore how to **disseminate** this plan through different team levels and **secure** stakeholder buy-in.

Formula

As a **[profession]** specializing in **[area of expertise/focus]** within the **[industry],** how can I guide my team in developing a plan for a new habit that will **[enhance workflow/boost results/improve performance]**? Provide an exhaustive and meticulous examination, incorporating innovative insights and inventive strategies for **[achieving this transformation/realizing this change/fostering this development]**. Also, explore how to **[disseminate/communicate]** this plan through different team levels and **[secure/obtain]** stakeholder buy-in.

Examples

Example 1: As a project manager specializing in agile methodologies within the healthcare industry, how can I guide my team in developing a plan for a new habit that will optimize overall performance? Provide an exhaustive and meticulous examination, incorporating innovative insights and inventive strategies for achieving this transformation. Also, explore how to disseminate this plan through different team levels and secure stakeholder buy-in.

Example 2: As a department head specializing in customer relations within the retail industry, how can I guide my team in developing a plan for a new habit aimed at improving customer satisfaction? Provide an exhaustive and meticulous examination, incorporating innovative insights and inventive strategies for achieving this transformation. Also, explore how to disseminate this plan through different team levels and secure stakeholder buy-in.

PROMPT No 102

Tags

Resources - Communication - Opportunity

Goal

To meticulously evaluate and articulate the types of resources, guidance, and infrastructure needed for your team to seize a new opportunity, aligning these needs with overarching organizational strategies.

Prompt

As a **project manager** specializing in **IT solutions** within the **tech industry**, provide an exhaustive and meticulous examination, incorporating innovative insights and inventive strategies for **assessing the specific support your team requires—such as manpower, skills training, or financial resources—to capitalize on a** new business opportunity. Additionally, delineate how to communicate these needs to **relevant stakeholders** for approval.

Formula

As a [profession] specializing in [area of expertise/focus] within the [industry], provide an exhaustive and meticulous examination, incorporating innovative insights and inventive strategies for **[assessing the specific support your team needs—be it in terms of manpower, skills training, or financial resources—to capitalize on a new business opportunity]**. Additionally, delineate how to communicate these needs to [relevant stakeholders/executive leadership/management] for approval.

Examples

Example 1: As a marketing director specializing in consumer goods within the retail industry, provide an exhaustive and meticulous examination, incorporating innovative insights and inventive strategies, to assess the specific support your creative team needs for launching a new advertising campaign. Additionally, delineate how to communicate these requirements to executive leadership for approval.

Example 2: As a scientific lead specializing in biotechnology within the pharmaceutical industry, provide an exhaustive and meticulous examination, incorporating innovative insights and inventive strategies, to assess the specific resources and expertise your research team requires to pursue a new drug discovery project. Additionally, delineate how to communicate these needs to the management for approval.

VALUES

PROMPT No 103

Tags

Priorities - Alignment - Team-Dynamics

Goal

To gain insights on specific methods to accurately pinpoint and engage in a thorough discussion about the top priorities and beliefs of team members, enhancing understanding and alignment within the team.

Prompt

In the context of **understanding what holds the most significance to my team members within their respective professions**, as a **Talent Development Specialist**, could you suggest specific methods to accurately pinpoint and engage in a thorough discussion about their top priorities and beliefs? I'm seeking this advice in a respectful and open-minded tone.

Formula

In the context of [contextual challenge/opportunity], as a [profession], could you suggest specific methods [I/Name/Role] can employ to accurately pinpoint and engage in a thorough discussion about the [desired outcome]? [I/They] am/are seeking this advice in a [tone of voice].

Examples

Example 1: In the context of understanding what holds the most significance to a project team within their respective roles, as a Team Coach, could you suggest specific methods a project manager can employ to accurately pinpoint and engage in a thorough discussion about their team's top priorities and beliefs? They are seeking this advice in a collaborative and patient tone.

Example 2: As an Executive Mentor, could you suggest specific methods I can employ to accurately pinpoint and engage in a thorough discussion about the top priorities and beliefs that hold the most significance to my sales team members within their respective roles? In the context of improving team alignment and performance, I'm seeking this advice in a supportive and respectful tone.

PROMPT No 104

Tags

Values - Relationships - Stakeholders

Goal

To furnish leaders with an insightful framework to discern the values that underline their team's interactions with each other and external stakeholders like clients. This will serve as the foundation for refining team dynamics, enhancing client relationships, and improving overall work culture.

Prompt

As an **Organizational Development Specialist** with specialization in **relational values** for the **financial sector**, could you guide me through **the process of uncovering the values that guide my team in establishing and sustaining productive relationships with colleagues and clients**? Include **techniques for qualitative and quantitative data gathering, types of questions to ask for self and peer assessments, and strategies to embed these values into organizational culture**. Make sure the guide covers **how to tie these values to key performance indicators and client satisfaction metrics**. Introduce unique angles and future-proof applications. Let's think about this step by step. Write using an **informative** tone and **factual** writing style.

Formula

As a **[profession]** with specialization in **[focus area]** for the **[industry]**, could you guide me through **[contextual challenge/opportunity]**? Include **[methods/techniques]**. Make sure the guide covers **[tools/frameworks]**. Introduce unique angles and future-proof applications. Let's think about this step by step. Write using a **[type]** tone and **[style]** writing style.

Examples

Example 1: As a Human Resources Consultant with a focus on workplace culture in the nonprofit sector, could you assist me in discerning the values that drive my team's interactions with each other and our donors? Include survey methods, types of reflective exercises, and frameworks to help define these values clearly. Make sure the guide incorporates how these values can be included in donor engagement strategies. Offer unique angles like the ethical considerations in nonprofit work. Let's dissect this carefully. Write using a compassionate tone and a human-centric writing style.

Example 2: As a Business Coach specializing in team dynamics for the retail industry, could you guide me in identifying the values that shape my team's relationships with co-workers and customers? Include observation techniques, examples of open-ended questions for team discussions, and action plans for ongoing value reinforcement. Make sure the guide suggests how to link these values to customer satisfaction and retention metrics. Discuss unique angles such as the impact of consumer psychology on value formation. Let's break this down methodically. Write using a commercial tone and a practical writing style.

PROMPT No 105

Tags

Behavior - Feedback - Nuanced

Goal

To elucidate a methodical approach for identifying scenarios or areas where the team is currently embodying their values, facilitating a deeper understanding and appreciation of value-driven practices within an organization.

Prompt

Act as a **Corporate Values Analyst** with a specialization in **Behavioral Assessment** within the **retail industry**. Could you guide me through **a systematic approach to discern the areas or situations where my team is currently honoring their values**? Please include **value-audit techniques, behavioral observation, and feedback collection methods**. Make sure to cover how to **create a conducive environment for value expression, evaluate the alignment of actions with stated values, and acknowledge and reinforce value-centric behaviors**. Delve into **avant-garde techniques to ensure a nuanced understanding of the manifestation of values in various team interactions and decision-making scenarios**. Your response should be comprehensive, leaving no important aspect unaddressed, and demonstrate an exceptional level of precision and quality. Let's think about this step by step. Write using an **insightful** tone and a **detail-oriented** writing style.

Formula

Act as a [profession] with a specialization in [area of expertise] within the [industry]. Could you guide me through [specific challenge/opportunity]? Please include [methods/techniques]. Make sure to cover how [key areas/topics]. Delve into [additional exploration]. Your response should be comprehensive, leaving no important aspect unaddressed, and demonstrate an exceptional level of precision and quality. Let's think about this step by step. Write using a [type] tone and a [style] writing style.

Examples

Example 1: Act as an Organizational Culture Expert with a specialization in Value Recognition within the hospitality industry. Could you guide me through an in-depth process to identify the scenarios or areas where my team is currently upholding their values? Please include value-mapping exercises, behavioral analysis, and team reflection sessions. Make sure to cover how to foster a culture of open communication, assess the congruence of actions with declared values, and celebrate value-driven accomplishments. Venture into pioneering methodologies to ensure a thorough comprehension of how values are being lived out in daily interactions and decision-making processes. Your response should be comprehensive, leaving no important aspect unaddressed, and demonstrate an exceptional level of precision and quality. Let's think about this step by step. Write using an encouraging tone and a reflective writing style.

Example 2: Act as a Team Dynamics Specialist with a specialization in Value Alignment within the financial services sector. Could you guide me through a structured approach to discern the instances or domains where my team is currently embodying their values? Please include value-assessment tools, behavioral indicators, and feedback loops. Make sure to cover how to establish a safe space for value articulation, gauge the alignment of team behaviors with organizational values, and recognize and reinforce value-centric practices. Explore innovative techniques to ensure a comprehensive understanding of the interplay between values, behaviors, and organizational outcomes. Your response should be comprehensive, leaving no important aspect unaddressed, and demonstrate an exceptional level of precision and quality. Let's think about this step by step. Write using a pragmatic tone and an analytical writing style.

PROMPT No 106

Tags

Integration - Reflective - Self-awareness

Goal

To facilitate a deeper exploration among team members regarding the alignment of their actions with their core values across different facets of life, thereby promoting a values-driven culture both within and outside the professional environment.

Prompt

Act as a **Life-Work Integration Specialist** with a specialization in **Values-Centric Engagement** within the **healthcare industry**. Could you guide me through **a process to help my team contemplate additional avenues through which they can honor their values in diverse aspects of their lives**? Please include **reflective exercises, discussion frameworks, and actionable strategies**. Make sure to cover how **to encourage self-awareness, foster open conversations around values, and inspire actions that resonate with their core beliefs**. Explore **innovative methods and alternative perspectives to nurture a holistic, values-honoring environment**. Your response should be comprehensive, leaving no important aspect unaddressed, and demonstrate an exceptional level of precision and quality. Let's think about this step by step. Write using an **inspiring** tone and a **solutions-focused** writing style.

Formula

Act as a [profession] with a specialization in [area of expertise] within the **[industry]**. Could you guide me through **[specific challenge/opportunity]**? Please include **[methods/techniques]**. Make sure to cover how **[key areas/topics]**. Explore **[additional exploration]**. Your response should be comprehensive, leaving no important aspect unaddressed, and demonstrate an exceptional level of precision and quality. Let's think about this step by step. Write using a **[type]** tone and a **[style]** writing style.

Examples

Example 1: Act as a Positive Psychology Coach with a specialization in Values Alignment within the technology sector. Could you guide me through an initiative to help my team explore additional manners to embody their values in varied life domains? Please include reflective practices, dialogue facilitation techniques, and actionable steps. Make sure to cover how to promote self-reflection, encourage value-centric dialogues, and inspire actions congruent with their values. Venture into novel approaches and diverse perspectives to create a culture that echoes shared values. Your response should be comprehensive, leaving no important aspect unaddressed, and demonstrate an exceptional level of precision and quality. Let's think about this step by step. Write using an empowering tone and a pragmatic writing style.

Example 2: Act as an Ethical Leadership Consultant with a specialization in Value-Based Action within the nonprofit sector. Could you guide me through a methodology to aid my team in discovering additional ways to honor their values across various life spheres? Please include introspective exercises, value-clarification workshops, and actionable plans. Make sure to cover how to foster value-awareness, facilitate value-focused discussions, and motivate value-aligned actions. Delve into cutting-edge methodologies and alternate viewpoints to nurture a value-honoring milieu. Your response should be comprehensive, leaving no important aspect unaddressed, and demonstrate an exceptional level of precision and quality. Let's think about this step by step. Write using a motivational tone and an instructive writing style.

PROMPT No 107

Tags

Openness - Fulfillment - HighPerformance

Goal

To help leaders implement a values-based strategy that promotes a culture of openness, high performance, and fulfillment within their teams. This involves not just explaining these values, but also embedding them into team dynamics and individual behaviors, thereby enhancing collective efficacy and individual satisfaction.

Prompt

As a **Leadership Development Coach** with a specialization in **organizational culture and values alignment** for the **technology sector**, could you guide me through **the methods to instill a specific set of values—openness, high performance, and fulfillment—in my team**? Include **strategies for the initial introduction of these values, interactive exercises to deepen understanding, and measures to sustain these values over time**. Ensure that the guide covers **frameworks or tools for assessing cultural alignment and methods** for **rewarding value-based actions**. Introduce unique angles and growth opportunities. Let's think about this step by step. Write using an **informative** tone and **factual** writing style.

Formula

As a **[profession]** with specialization in **[focus area]** for the **[industry]**, could you guide me through **[contextual challenge/opportunity]**? Include **[methods/techniques]**. Ensure that the guide covers **[tools/frameworks]** for **[desired outcomes]**. Introduce unique angles and growth opportunities. Let's think about this step by step. Write using a **[type]** tone and **[style]** writing style.

Examples

Example 1: As an Organizational Psychologist with a focus on team dynamics for the healthcare industry, could you guide me through the techniques to infuse values of patient-centered care, teamwork, and job satisfaction among my nursing staff? Provide suggestions for interactive workshops, discussions that encourage sharing, and reinforcement mechanisms. Make sure the guide includes psychometric tests like DISC or MBTI for gauging alignment and ways to celebrate value-driven wins. Introduce untapped methods and innovative growth strategies. Let's break this down systematically. Write using an empathetic tone and a constructive writing style.

Example 2: As a Corporate Trainer specializing in value-driven leadership for the marketing industry, could you walk me through the strategy to instill a culture of innovation, agility, and professional development in my team? Include detailed plans for launch meetings, brainstorming sessions, and sustainability tactics. Ensure that the guide elaborates on KPIs aligned with these values and techniques for regular values audits. Explore unconventional approaches and emerging opportunities. Let's dissect this incrementally. Write using an enthusiastic tone and an inspirational writing style.

WEAKNESS

PROMPT No 108

Tags

GoalAchievement - Weaknesses - PersonalGrowth

Goal

To obtain a comprehensive, actionable framework for identifying personal weaknesses that need to be addressed for goal achievement, as well as outlining the initial steps for improvement. The aim is to enhance self-awareness, personal development, and facilitate a structured approach to goal attainment.

Prompt

As a **Personal Development Coach** in the **finance industry**, could you provide a **comprehensive plan** detailing the **methods I** can use to identify which weaknesses **I** need to work on to achieve **my career goals**? Additionally, outline the **initial steps** for improvement. Segment your insights into distinct modules, each supported by **evidence from reputable journals**. Investigate unexpected avenues and creative pathways. Let's dissect this carefully. Write using a **consultative** tone and a **narrative** writing style.

Formula

As a [profession] in the [industry], could you provide a [comprehensive plan/thorough toolkit/detailed blueprint] detailing the [methods/tactics/strategies] [I/Name/Role] can use to identify which weaknesses [I/they] need to work on to achieve [my/their] [specific/short-term/long-term] goals? Additionally, outline the [initial steps/first actions/immediate measures] for improvement. Segment your insights into distinct modules, each supported by [evidence from/references from/data from] [reputable journals/credible research/authoritative publications]. Investigate unexpected avenues and creative pathways. Let's dissect this carefully. Write using a [consultative/empathetic/balanced] tone and a [narrative/nuanced/concise] writing style.

Examples

Example 1: As a Career Development Consultant in the healthcare sector, could you provide a detailed blueprint outlining the methods a nurse can use to identify which weaknesses they need to work on to achieve their professional development goals? Additionally, outline the first actions for improvement. Segment your insights into distinct modules, each authenticated by corroborative evidence from credible sources. Explore unconventional approaches and diverse viewpoints. Let's examine each dimension meticulously. Write using a balanced tone and a concise writing style.

Example 2: As a Life Coach in the entertainment industry, could you provide a thorough toolkit outlining the tactics an actor can use to identify which weaknesses they need to work on to achieve their performance goals? Additionally, outline the immediate measures for improvement. Segment your insights into distinct modules, each endorsed with data from verified academic publications. Unearth hidden gems and non-traditional methods. Let's dissect this carefully. Write using an empathetic tone and a nuanced writing style.

PROMPT No 109

Tags

Weaknesses - Conversation - Risk-Assessment

Goal

To equip business leaders with the necessary tools to have a constructive discussion with their teams about understanding the potential downsides of their weaknesses. This conversation should highlight the link between specific weaknesses and potential troubles or challenges, thereby motivating team members to recognize the need for improvement.

Prompt

As a **Leadership Development Coach** specializing in **risk assessment and mitigation** for the **software development industry**, could you guide me through **facilitating a conversation with my team about how their weaknesses could lead to troubles or challenges**? Please outline **the conversation initiation techniques, the types of questions to ask to foster self-awareness, and methods for creating a comfortable and non-judgmental environment**. Make sure to cover **techniques for peer-to-peer feedback and incorporating performance metrics to quantify the impact of these weaknesses**. Introduce unique angles and forward-thinking opportunities. Let's think about this step by step. Write using an **informative** tone and **factual** writing style.

Formula

As a [profession] specializing in [focus area] for the [industry], could you guide me through [context of conversation]? Please outline [initiation techniques/questions/methods]. Make sure to cover [additional elements like feedback or metrics]. Introduce unique angles and [type of opportunities]. Let's think about this step by step. Write using a [type] tone and [style] writing style.

Examples

Example 1: As an Organizational Psychologist with a focus on problem-solving for the manufacturing industry, could you guide me through initiating a dialogue with my team about how their problem-solving weaknesses could result in manufacturing defects or delays? Please provide techniques for setting the stage, questions that delve into their thought processes, and ways to establish a safe environment for candid discussion. Ensure the guide incorporates self-assessment tools such as SWOT analysis and ways to encourage peer review. Introduce out-of-the-box strategies and untapped potentials. Let's analyze this methodically. Write using a supportive tone and accessible writing style.

Example 2: As a Business Communications Expert specializing in internal relations for the retail sector, could you walk me through holding a conversation with my team about how weaknesses in communication could lead to misunderstandings or lost sales? Please share methodologies for opening the conversation, types of questions that drive self-reflection, and methods for ensuring psychological safety during the discussion. Make sure the guide includes tips for using real-world scenarios and peer-to-peer feedback to make the impact more relatable. Introduce innovative ideas and visionary opportunities. Let's dissect this carefully. Write using a persuasive tone and direct writing style.

PROMPT No 110

Tags

Assessment - Career - Recognition

Goal

To gain specific techniques or approaches that can be utilized to effectively identify and assess any signs or indications of weaknesses in the career or professional performance of a team, ensuring accurate recognition and evaluation of these weaknesses.

Prompt

As a **Leadership Development Consultant**, adopting a **supportive and analytical tone**, could you provide specific techniques or approaches that can be utilized to **effectively identify and assess any signs or indications of weaknesses** in the career or professional performance of **my team**? Please provide detailed and comprehensive suggestions that will **ensure accurate recognition and evaluation of these weaknesses**.

Formula

As a [profession], adopting a [tone of voice], could you provide specific techniques or approaches that can be utilized to [contextual challenge/opportunity] in the career or professional performance of [my/their] [team/group/department]? Please provide detailed and comprehensive suggestions that will [desired outcome].

Examples

Example 1: As a Human Resources Consultant, adopting a professional and empathetic tone, could you provide specific techniques or approaches that can be utilized to effectively identify and assess any signs or indications of weaknesses in the career or professional performance of our sales team? Please provide detailed and comprehensive suggestions that will ensure accurate recognition and evaluation of these weaknesses.

Example 2: As a Team Coach, adopting a constructive and encouraging tone, could you provide specific techniques or approaches that can be utilized to effectively identify and assess any signs or indications of weaknesses in the career or professional performance of my engineering team? Please provide detailed and comprehensive suggestions that will ensure accurate recognition and evaluation of these weaknesses.

PROMPT No 111

Tags

Transformation - Confidence - Communication

Goal

To guide you in recognizing the value of mastering a current weakness, and how to understand the potential benefits and transformation that can result from this self-improvement. The prompt is aimed at both self-reflection and action planning, inspiring you to not only identify weaknesses but also to see the potential in transforming those areas.

Prompt

Act as a **Personal Development Coach** specializing in the **public sector**. If I were to **identify** a **current weakness** in my **professional life** and become **truly masterful** in that **area**, what could the **implications** be? How might it **impact** my **confidence, career trajectory, relationships, or overall satisfaction**? What **strategies** can I employ to transform the weakness of **lack of communication skills** into a **strength**? How can I **track progress** and **maintain** motivation in this **journey**? Respond to each question separately. Let's consider each facet of this topic. Write using an **inspirational** tone and **engaging** writing style.

Formula

Act as a [profession] specializing in the [sector], if I were to [identify/recognize/determine] a [current/existing/present] [weakness/flaw/shortcoming] in my [professional/personal/individual] life and become [truly/completely/absolutely] [masterful/expert/skilled] in that [area/field/aspect], what could the [implications/consequences/ramifications] be? How might it [impact/affect/influence] my [confidence/career/relationships/overall satisfaction]? What [strategies/tools/methodologies] can I [employ/use/apply] to [transform/convert/change] the [weakness/flaw/shortcoming] of [insert weakness/flaw/shortcoming] into a [strength/asset/virtue]? How can I [track/monitor/observe] [progress/advancement/development] and [maintain/keep/sustain] [motivation/enthusiasm/drive] in this [journey/process/endeavor]? Respond to each question separately. Let's consider each facet of this topic. Write using a [type] tone and [style] writing style.

Examples

Example 1: Act as a Leadership Trainer specializing in the tech industry. If I could pinpoint a current weakness in my leadership style and develop genuine mastery in that domain, what transformations could occur? How would it influence my team's performance, my personal growth, or the innovation within my organization? What specific actions, resources, or mentors could I seek to cultivate this mastery? How can I ensure sustained growth and passion in this area? Respond to each question separately. Let's dissect this carefully. Write using a confident tone and analytical writing style.

Example 2: Act as a Performance Coach specializing in the healthcare industry. If I recognize a current area of weakness in my medical practice and become adept in that specialty, what might the benefits be? How could it enhance patient care, professional satisfaction, or interdisciplinary collaboration? What training, support networks, or ongoing learning paths might aid in this transformation? How can I celebrate successes and stay inspired in this developmental journey? Respond to each question separately. Let's analyze this piece by piece. Write using a compassionate tone and informative writing style.

Final Words

In the domain of coaching, mentoring, and leadership, navigating the complexities requires a disciplined approach. This book aims to be an instrumental guide, leveraging artificial intelligence and prompt engineering to provide actionable insights for those in any profession. I have presented a curated list of prompts, each serving a specific objective: to clarify roles, define leadership strategies, and optimize coaching techniques, to name a few.

The scope of this book goes beyond a mere compilation of prompts. My goal is to impart a strategic mindset for interpreting challenges as opportunities, seeing barriers as milestones for growth, and viewing the future as a dynamic environment that can be strategically managed.

For the reader who began with skepticism, I hope you conclude this book with a newfound confidence, equipped with a toolkit that elevates your professional standing. For the experienced practitioner, may the methods and strategies here serve to refine your existing approaches.

This journey, while individual in nature, is set against the backdrop of collective human experience. Artificial intelligence serves as a bridge to this collective wisdom, streamlining the path toward your professional and personal development objectives.

In summary, this book aims to leave you not just prepared but empowered. As you close this chapter and move forward in your career, be reminded that each decision and action point offers an opportunity for growth and leadership. This is not just preparation; it is empowerment for transformative impact.

The challenges you face should be viewed as opportunities for demonstrating your leadership and expertise. I encourage you to approach these with a strategic focus, grounded in the knowledge and insights you have gained from this book.

I wish you all the best.

Mauricio

PS: Enjoyed your book? Scan the QR code to quickly leave a review where you purchased it. Your feedback is invaluable!

APPENDIXES

Appendix No 1

Sign-In to Chatbots

1,1. Chat GPT

Step 1: Visit ChatGPT on https://chat.openai.com/chat Click on "Sign Up" and then create your account.

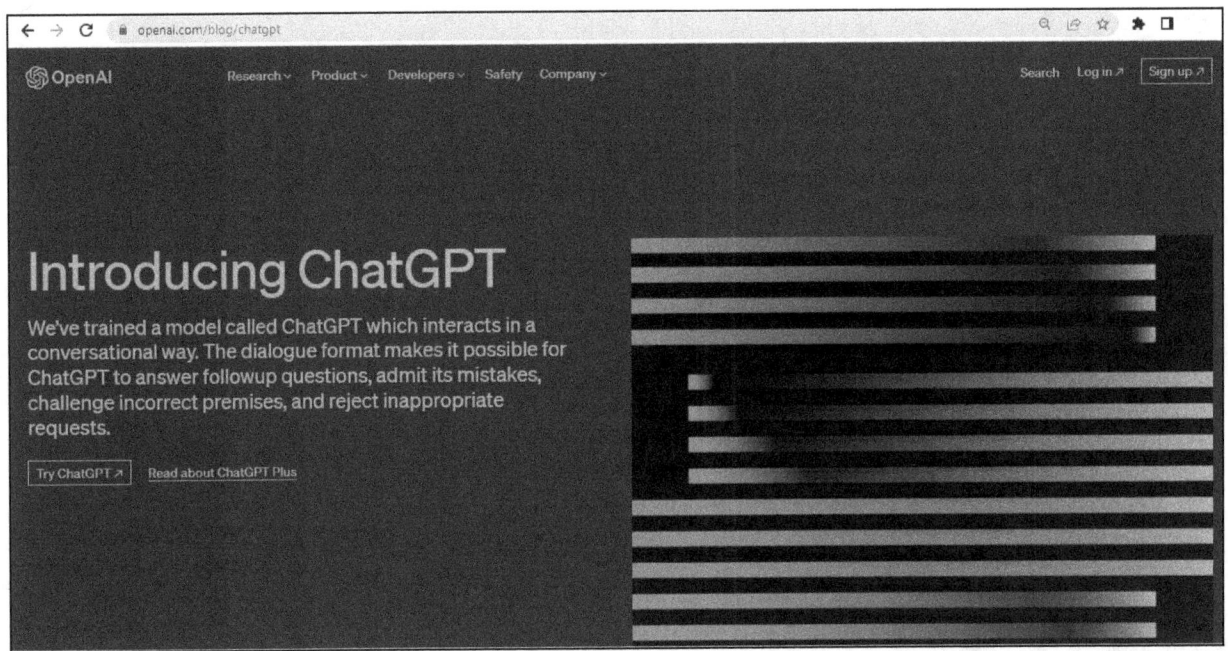

Step 2: Verify your Account. You'd have to enter your details, verify your email and give an OTP you'll receive on your phone.

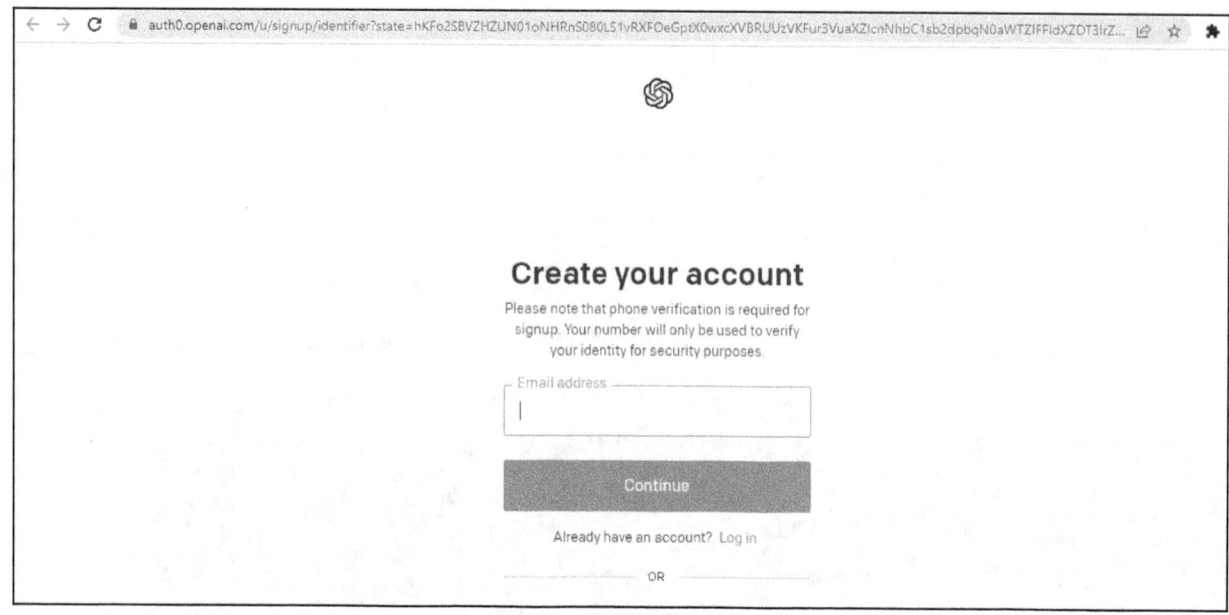

Once done, you'd have access to the free version of ChatGPT

As of April 2023, ChatGPT 3.5 is free to use and ChatGPT-4 costs $20 per month. As a beginner, you can easily test your skills on the free version.

This is how it looks:

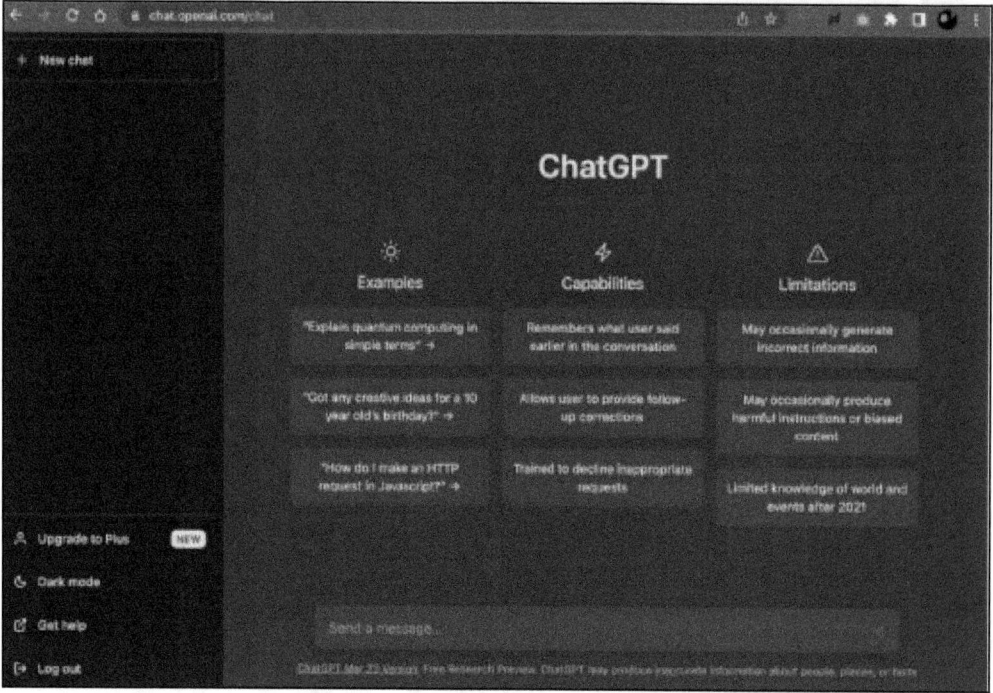

At the very bottom is where you'd chat:

You can now ask GPT anything you want, and it'll give you the desired result

Note: The procedure outlined was developed based on the instructions available at the time of writing. If you require further assistance with signing up for ChatGPT, please scan this QR code:

1.2. Bing Chat

Step 1: Go to the Microsoft website (www.microsoft.com).

Locate the download page for Edge or look for "Microsoft Edge" in the search bar. If you don't want to download Microsoft Edge, go directly to Step 6. For better results, we recommend using Microsoft Edge.

Step 2: Click the download button and choose the version that fits your system.

Step 3: Once downloaded, open the setup file.

Step 4: A User Account Control dialog box will appear – click "Yes" to grant permission.

The installation wizard will guide you through a series of prompts and options. Review them carefully.

Step 5: To open Microsfot Edge, press Win + R on the keyboard to open the Run window.
In the Open field, type "microsoft-edge:" and press Enter on the keyboard or click or tap OK. Microsoft Edge is now open.

Step 6: Head to bing.com/chat

Step 7: From the pop-up that appears, click 'Start chatting'

Step 8: Enter the email address for the Microsoft account you'd like to use and click 'Next'.

If you don't have one, click 'Create one!' just under the text box and follow the instructions. Enter your password when prompted and click Next. From the following screen, choose whether you'd like to stay signed in or not. Click 'Chat Now'

Step 9: Choose your conversation style. If you've never used it before, it's best to stick with 'More Balanced'

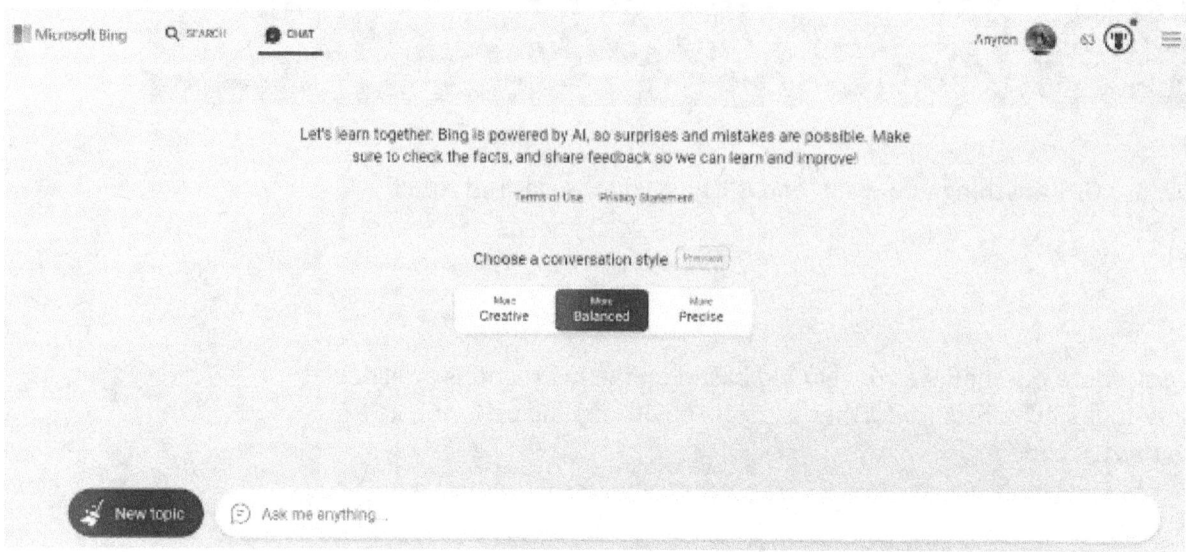

That's it! You can now start chatting.

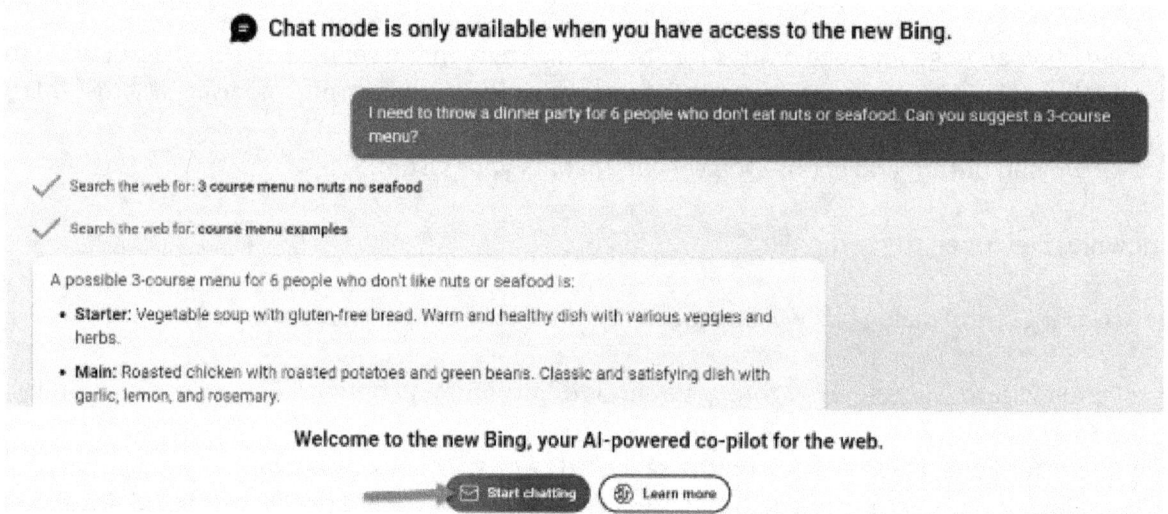

Note: The procedure outlined was developed based on the instructions available at the time of writing. If you require assistance with signing up for Bing Chat, please scan this QR code:

1.3. Google Bard

Step 1: Go to bard.google.com. Select Try Bard. Accept Google Bard Terms of Service

110

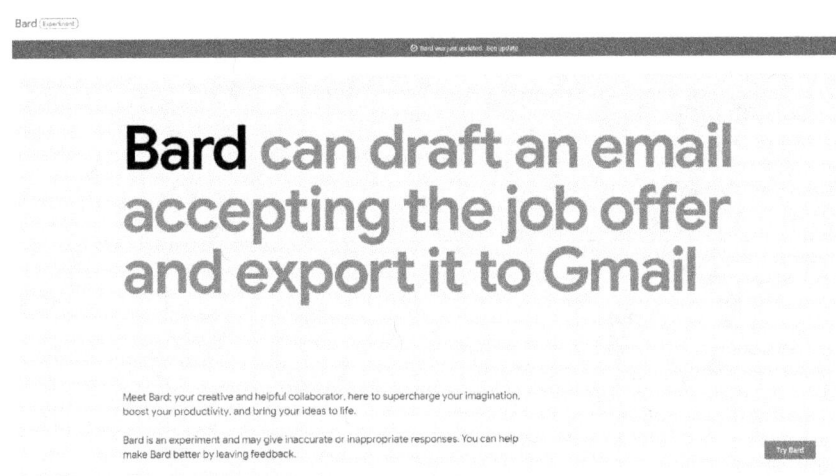

Step 2: Go to "Sign in"

Step 3: Enter a query or search term and then hit enter.

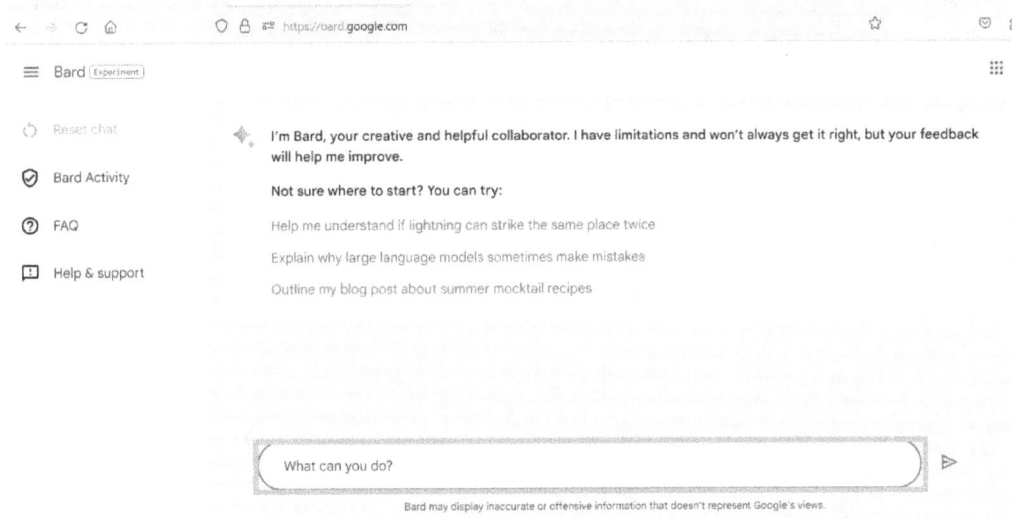

Wait for the AI to respond. You can then either continue the conversation or select Google It to use the traditional search engine.

Note: The procedure outlined was developed based on the instructions available at the time of writing. If you require assistance with signing up for Google Bard, please scan this QR code:

1.4. Meta LLaMA

Getting the Models

Step 1: Go to https://ai.meta.com/resources/models-and-libraries/llama-downloads/

Step 2: Fill the form with your information.

Step 3: Accept their license (if you agree with it)

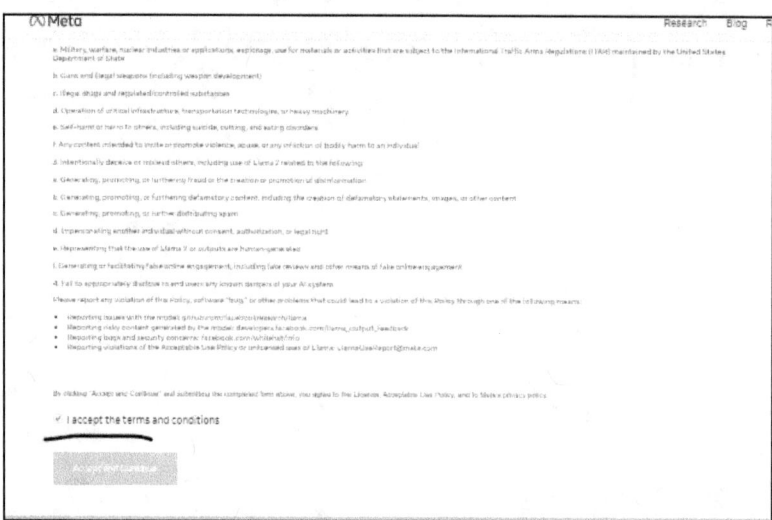

Step 4: Once your request is approved, you will receive a signed URL over email.

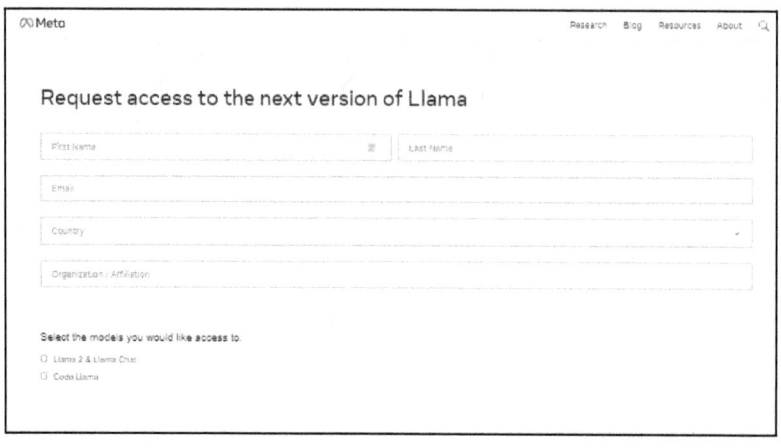

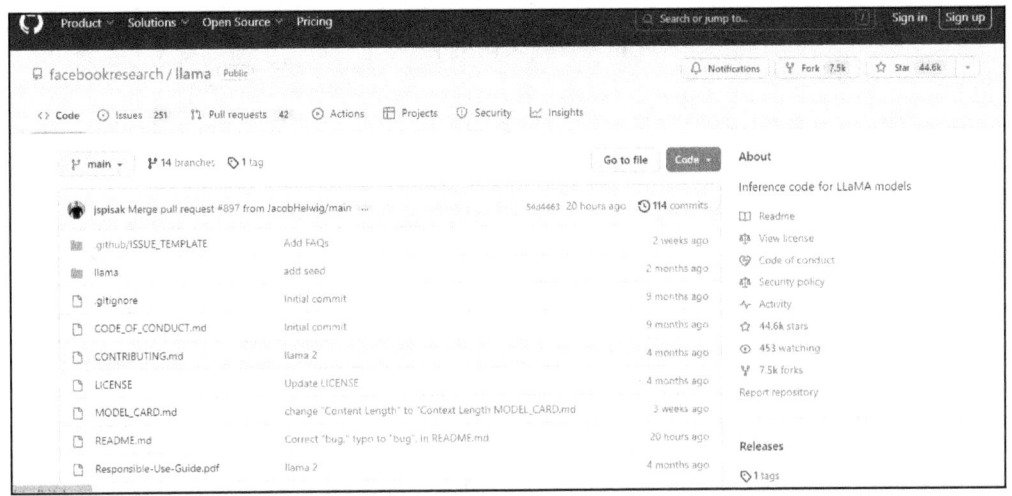

Step 5: Clone the Llama 2 repository (go to https://github.com/facebookresearch/llama).

Step 6: Run the download.sh script, passing the URL provided when prompted to start the download. Keep in mind that the links expire after 24 hours and a certain amount of downloads. If you start seeing errors such as 403: Forbidden, you can always re-request a link.

Appendix No 2

Follow-up Prompts

There are 1100 prompts that you can use as follow-ups in order to get more specific or revised information from ChatGPT and other Chatbots. Don't forget to tailor these prompts to your specific circumstances and to the response you previously received from the Chatbot.

Each of these prompt types serves a different purpose and can be used effectively in different scenarios. Depending on the context and the intended outcome, one type of prompt may be more suitable than another.

These prompts are divided into eleven distinct categories, each tailored to specific conversational needs: Generic, Enhancement, Clarification, Probing, Critical Thinking, Instructional, Exploration, Comparison, Summarization, Evaluation, and Hypothetical.

To have access to 1100 follow-up prompts, please scan this QR code:

Appendix No 3

A Beginner's Step-by-Step Guide to Using ChatGPT

If you're new to ChatGPT, don't fret. This guide is designed to walk you through its use, step by step. By the end, you'll have a solid grasp of how to harness the power of this incredible tool.

Step 1: Accessing the Platform

Visit OpenAI's Platform: Head to OpenAI's official website: ChatGPT [openai.com]

Sign Up/Log In: If you don't have an account, you'll need to sign up. If you already have one, simply log in.

Step 2: Navigating the Interface

Dashboard: This is your central hub, where you can access various tools and see your usage stats.

Start a New Session: To interact with ChatGPT, start a new session or use a predefined platform depending on the current interface.

Step 3: Interacting with ChatGPT

Input Field: This is where you'll type or paste the prompts from our book.

Submit: Once you've entered your prompt, press 'Enter' or click the 'Submit' button.

Review Output: ChatGPT will generate a response. Take a moment to read and understand it.

Step 4: Refining Your Interaction

Being Specific: If you need specific information or a particular type of response, make your prompts more detailed.

Iterate: If the first response isn't what you're looking for, tweak your prompt and try again.

Step 5: Utilizing the Prompts from This Book

Choose a Prompt: Browse the book's prompt section and select one that aligns with your current needs.

Input: Copy and paste or type the chosen prompt into ChatGPT's input field.

Customization: Feel free to adjust the prompts to be more specific to your situation.

Step 6: Safety and Best Practices

Sensitive Information: Never share sensitive personal information, such as Social Security numbers or bank details, with ChatGPT or any online platform.

Understanding Outputs: Remember, while ChatGPT can produce human-like responses, it doesn't understand context in the same way humans do. Always review its advice with a critical eye.

Step 7: Exploring Advanced Features

As you become more comfortable with ChatGPT:

Experiment: Play around with different types of prompts to see the diverse responses you can get.

Integrate with Other Tools: There are several third-party tools and platforms that have integrated ChatGPT. Explore these to maximize your work.

Step 8: Stay Updated

Technology, especially in the AI field, evolves rapidly. Periodically check OpenAI's official channels for updates, new features, or changes to the platform.

By following this guide, even the most tech-averse individuals will find themselves comfortably navigating and interacting with ChatGPT. As we delve deeper into the book and introduce specific prompts tailored for your work you'll be equipped with the knowledge to make the most of them.

Here is our "*Elevate Your Productivity Using ChatGPT*" Guide: To access this guide to boost your efficiency and productivity, please scan this QR code.

Appendix No 4

Mentoring, Coaching, and Leadership Professionals

This list encompasses professions pivotal in nurturing growth, leadership, and collaboration in work settings. They play crucial roles in guiding, training, and inspiring individuals towards achieving personal and organizational objectives.

1. Mentor: Provides guidance, support, and wisdom to less experienced individuals for personal and professional growth.
2. Coach: Assists in developing specific skills, improving performance, and achieving defined objectives through structured guidance.
3. Leader: Guides, inspires, and influences a group towards achieving common goals, fostering positive organizational culture.
4. Executive Coach: Assists executives in honing leadership skills, achieving goals, and navigating career transitions.
5. Life Coach: Guides individuals in personal development, goal-setting, and achieving life balance.
6. Career Counselor: Provides advice on career exploration, development strategies, and job search.
7. Organizational Consultant: Aids organizations in improving performance, culture, and change management.
8. Training and Development Manager: Plans, directs, and coordinates programs to enhance employee skills.
9. Human Resources Manager: Oversees recruitment, employee relations, and organizational development.
10. Management Consultant: Advises on business strategies, problem-solving, and organizational improvements.
11. Leadership Development Specialist: Creates programs to develop leadership capabilities within organizations.
12. Performance Coach: Helps individuals improve performance and achieve professional objectives.
13. Business Coach: Guides entrepreneurs in business growth, strategy, and problem-solving.
14. Conflict Resolution Specialist: Aids in resolving disputes and improving communication in workplaces.
15. Executive Search Consultant: Assists organizations in identifying and recruiting executive leadership talent.
16. Team Building Specialist: Designs and facilitates activities to enhance team cohesion.
17. Corporate Trainer: Provides training to improve employee skills and knowledge.
18. Communication Coach: Improves interpersonal communication skills within professional settings.
19. Industrial-Organizational Psychologist: Applies psychological principles to improve workplace dynamics.
20. Change Management Consultant: Guides organizations through change with strategies to ensure smooth transitions.
21. Culture Development Consultant: Aids in cultivating a positive, productive organizational culture.
22. Educational Consultant: Advises on educational strategies, curriculum development, and leadership.
23. Talent Development Specialist: Identifies and nurtures employee talents for organizational growth.
24. Learning and Development Specialist: Designs and implements training programs to promote employee growth and organizational success.
25. Supply Chain Manager: Oversees the end-to-end supply chain process to ensure efficiency and effectiveness.
26. Negotiation Consultant: Aids in enhancing negotiation skills and strategies.
27. Mediator: Facilitates resolution of disputes in a neutral manner.
28. Customer Service Trainer: Improves customer interaction skills of service teams.

29. Process Improvement Consultant: Aids in enhancing operational processes for greater efficiency and productivity.
30. Entrepreneurship Advisor: Guides individuals in launching and growing their own businesses.

Appendix No 5

Specializations for Mentors, Coaches and Leaders

1. This compilation presents specialized roles integral to fostering excellence, innovation, and resilience within professional landscapes, offering tailored guidance and support to propel individuals and businesses toward their aspirations.
2. Leadership: Enhancing skills for leading teams and organizations effectively.
3. Performance: Boosting individual or team productivity and output.
4. Career: Navigating career progression and transitions.
5. Sales: Increasing sales proficiency and results.
6. Marketing: Crafting and executing marketing strategies.
7. Strategy: Formulating and applying long-term business plans.
8. Innovation: Fostering creative thinking and new ideas.
9. Culture: Shaping positive organizational values and practices.
10. Conflict Resolution: Managing and resolving disputes effectively.
11. Communication Skills: Improving sharing and receiving of information.
12. Emotional Intelligence: Understanding and managing emotions for improved interactions.
13. Team Dynamics: Strengthening team cooperation and function.
14. Change Leadership: Guiding successful organizational change.
15. Diversity and Inclusion: Building respectful, diverse work environments.
16. Work-Life Balance: Balancing professional responsibilities with personal life.
17. Organizational Development: Enhancing organizational structures and efficiency.
18. Time Management: Prioritizing tasks and managing time wisely.
19. Customer Success: Ensuring clients achieve their desired outcomes.
20. Negotiation Skills: Reaching agreements effectively and advantageously.
21. Personal Branding: Crafting and communicating a personal image.
22. Corporate Governance: Directing company management and policies.
23. Business Ethics: Promoting ethical professional conduct.
24. Financial Coaching for Executives: Managing company finances and economic strategy.
25. Talent Development: Growing employee skills and career paths.
26. Digital Transformation: Integrating digital technology into all business areas.
27. Entrepreneurship: Starting and growing new business ventures.
28. Global Leadership: Leading across diverse cultures and markets.
29. Sustainability Leadership: Integrating eco-friendly practices into business.
30. Mindfulness and Well-being: Promoting mental health and mindfulness practices.

Appendix No 6

Tones

Tone reflects the emotional stance towards the subject or audience, impacting engagement and receptivity. In coaching or leadership, the right tone fosters trust, motivation, and effective communication, aligning with growth-oriented goals.

1. Motivational: Inspiring action and positivity towards achieving goals.
2. Empathetic: Demonstrating understanding and compassion towards others' experiences.
3. Authoritative: Exuding confidence and expertise in guiding others.
4. Inspirational: Provoking thought and encouraging higher aspirations.
5. Supportive: Offering encouragement and backing during challenges.
6. Reflective: Encouraging contemplation and self-assessment.
7. Directive: Providing clear, actionable guidance.
8. Analytical: Examining situations critically and logically.
9. Advisory: Offering suggestions based on expertise.
10. Challenging: Encouraging stretching beyond comfort zones.
11. Respectful: Honoring individuals' values, thoughts, and feelings.
12. Humorous: Adding levity to engage and ease tension.
13. Socratic: Encouraging critical thinking through questioning.
14. Constructive: Providing feedback for growth and improvement.
15. Patient: Showing understanding and tolerance during learning processes.
16. Optimistic: Highlighting the positive and potential success.
17. Realistic: Providing a practical and sensible perspective.
18. Encouraging: Boosting morale and self-efficacy.
19. Appreciative: Acknowledging efforts and achievements.
20. Reassuring: Alleviating concerns and instilling confidence.
21. Inquisitive: Encouraging exploration and curiosity.
22. Observational: Noting and reflecting on behaviors and outcomes.
23. Persuasive: Convincing others towards a certain viewpoint.
24. Resilient: Demonstrating toughness and adaptability in adversity.
25. Visionary: Focusing on long-term potential and broader horizons.
26. Collegial: Promoting a sense of partnership and teamwork.
27. Energizing: Infusing enthusiasm and vigor.
28. Compassionate: Showing care and understanding in dealing with others.
29. Professional: Maintaining a formal and respectful demeanor.
30. Mindful: Demonstrating awareness and consideration.

Appendix No 7

Writing Styles

Writing style denotes how ideas are expressed, encompassing word choice and narrative flow. In coaching, mentoring, and leadership, an apt style clarifies concepts, provides guidance, and facilitates meaningful exploration of ideas.

1. Expository: Explaining facts and information clearly and straightforwardly.
2. Descriptive: Painting a vivid picture to convey a particular scenario or idea.
3. Narrative: Telling a story or recounting events to convey lessons or insights.
4. Persuasive: Arguing a point or encouraging a particular action or mindset.
5. Concise: Delivering information in a brief, direct manner.
6. Analytical: Dissecting information to understand and convey underlying principles.
7. Reflective: Encouraging introspection and consideration of past experiences.
8. Dialogic: Engaging in a two-way conversation to explore ideas.
9. Illustrative: Using examples and anecdotes to clarify points.
10. Instructive: Providing detailed guidance or instructions.
11. Interpretive: Explaining and making sense of complex concepts.
12. Comparative: Analyzing similarities and differences between concepts.
13. Argumentative: Making a case for a particular stance or action.
14. Problem-Solution: Identifying issues and proposing solutions.
15. Evaluative: Assessing the value or effectiveness of certain practices.
16. Journalistic: Reporting facts in an objective, straightforward manner.
17. Exploratory: Delving into topics to discover new insights or perspectives.
18. Contemplative: Encouraging deep thought on certain topics.
19. Case Study: Delving into real-world examples to extract lessons.
20. Research-based: Grounding discourse in empirical evidence.
21. Informal: Adopting a casual, accessible approach.
22. Formal: Adhering to professional language and structure.
23. Technical: Utilizing specialized terminology relevant to the field.
24. Conceptual: Exploring ideas at a high level.
25. Practical: Focusing on actionable advice and real-world application.
26. Empirical: Relying on observation and experience.
27. Theoretical: Delving into theories and abstract concepts.
28. Storyboard: Unfolding ideas through a sequenced narrative.
29. Interactive: Encouraging active engagement from the reader.
30. Scenario-based: Outlining hypothetical situations to explore concepts.

Appendix No 8

Tags

	Chapter	**Tag 1**	**Tag 2**	**Tag 3**
Prompt 1	Accountability	RemoteWork	Self-Accountability	Commitment
Prompt 2	Accountability	Strategic Plan	Team Motivation	Revenue Alignment
Prompt 3	Accountability	Client Acquisition	Business Development	Detailed Strategy
Prompt 4	Accountability	Effective Communication	Team Cooperation	Initiative Implementation
Prompt 5	Accountability	Relationship Maintenance	Collaborative Strategies	Professional Interaction
Prompt 6	Awareness	False Assumptions	Insightful Leadership	Self-Reflection
Prompt 7	Awareness	Goal-Setting	Prioritization Strategies	Task Management
Prompt 8	Awareness	Project Preparation	Team Equipping	Effective Tackling
Prompt 9	Awareness	Effective Communication	Team Understanding	Self-Awareness Enhancement
Prompt 10	Awareness	Alignment	Beliefs	Performance
Prompt 11	Awareness	Leadership	Action	Productivity
Prompt 12	Belief	Verification	Evidence	Strategy
Prompt 13	Belief	Self-awareness	Improvement	Challenge
Prompt 14	Belief	Identification	Covert	Motivations
Prompt 15	Belief	Stakeholders	Interaction	Performance
Prompt 16	Belief	Viewpoints	Reevaluation	Diversity
Prompt 17	Belief	Responsibilities	Clarity	Productivity
Prompt 18	Challenge	Uncertainty	Capabilities	Support
Prompt 19	Challenge	Attitudes	Benefit	Mindset
Prompt 20	Challenge	Motivation	Inspiration	Challenges
Prompt 21	Challenge	Thriving	Adaptation	Insights
Prompt 22	Challenge	Diverse-Thinking	Problem-Solving	Leadership
Prompt 23	Change	Mindset-Change	Productivity	Organizational-Development
Prompt 24	Change	Celebration	Team-Morale	Appreciation
Prompt 25	Change	Proposal-Development	Positive-Change	Work-Habits
Prompt 26	Change	Assessment	Improvement	Team-Development
Prompt 27	Commitment	Communication	Promotion	Motivation
Prompt 28	Creativity	Satisfaction	Engagement	Productivity
Prompt 29	Creativity	Responsibility	Service	Contribution
Prompt 30	Decisions	Timelines	Realism	Performance
Prompt 31	Decisions	Ethics	Decision-Making	Alignment
Prompt 32	Excitement	Professional-Development	C-suite	Effectiveness
Prompt 33	Excitement	Rejuvenation	Support	Energy
Prompt 34	Excitement	Conflict-Resolution	Relationship	Positivity

Prompt 35	Fear	Empathy	Anxiety	Workplace
Prompt 36	Fear	Resilience	Inspiration	Support
Prompt 37	Feelings	Emotional-Intelligence	Leadership	Responsiveness
Prompt 38	Feelings	Dissatisfaction	Morale	Promotion
Prompt 39	Feelings	Roles	Emotional-Intelligence	Cohesion
Prompt 40	Flow	Metrics	Productivity	Influence
Prompt 41	Flow	Diversity	Engagement	Fulfillment
Prompt 42	Fulfillment	Attributes	Leadership	Empathy
Prompt 43	Goals	Evaluation	Growth	KPIs
Prompt 44	Goals	Collaboration	Frameworks	Cohesiveness
Prompt 45	Goals	Assessment	Performance	Accountability
Prompt 46	Goals	Team-Reflection	Motivation	Goal-Setting
Prompt 47	Habits	Obstacles	Methodologies	Strategy
Prompt 48	Habits	Communication	ActiveListening	Self-awareness
Prompt 49	Learning	Energy	Motivation	Leadership
Prompt 50	Learning	Opportunities	Vigilance	Identification
Prompt 51	Learning	Motivation	Reflection	Positivity
Prompt 52	Learning	Reflection	ProjectManagement	Self-awareness
Prompt 53	Learning	TalentDevelopment	Alignment	Interests
Prompt 54	Learning	Investigation	Failure	Improvement
Prompt 55	Learning	Learning	Reflection	Actionability
Prompt 56	Listening	Performance-Enhancement	Conversation	Improvement
Prompt 57	Listening	Resilience	Mindfulness	Strategy
Prompt 58	Mindset	Leadership	Transparency	Accountability
Prompt 59	Mindset	Vulnerability	Well-being	Psychological-Safety
Prompt 60	Mindset	Talent	Identification	Delegation
Prompt 61	Mindset	Transparency	Role-Clarity	Objectives
Prompt 62	Options	Proactive	Collaboration	Bankruptcy
Prompt 63	Options	Resilience	Challenge-Management	Personal-Growth
Prompt 64	Options	Decision-making	Frameworks	Participation
Prompt 65	Performance	Adaptability	Growth	Accounting
Prompt 66	Performance	Mindset	Transformation	Support
Prompt 67	Performance	Goal-Attainment	Modification	Performance
Prompt 68	Preferences	Rapport	Creativity	Engagement
Prompt 69	Priorities	Productivity	Diagnostics	Behavior Analysis
Prompt 70	Priorities	Strategy	Decision-Making	Prioritization
Prompt 71	Progress	Recognition	Morale	Engagement
Prompt 72	Progress	Reflection	Self-awareness	Goals
Prompt 73	Purpose	Self-Perception	Dialogue	Performance
Prompt 74	Purpose	Goal-setting	Articulation	Clarity

Prompt 75	Purpose	Career Development	Software	Aspirations
Prompt 76	Purpose	Leadership	Encouragement	Purpose
Prompt 77	Relationships	Fulfillment	Implementation	Clients
Prompt 78	Relationships	Self-awareness	Relationships	Dynamics
Prompt 79	Relationships	Self-awareness	Engagement	Motivating
Prompt 80	Relationships	Creativity	Innovation	Framework
Prompt 81	Relationships	Relationship	Diagnostics	Constructive
Prompt 82	Relationships	Presence	Engagement	Meetings
Prompt 83	Relationships	Obstacles	Self-Assessment	Nurturing
Prompt 84	Relationships	Confidence	Empowerment	Leadership
Prompt 85	Relationships	Role-Optimization	Responsibilities	Personal-Growth
Prompt 86	Relationships	Support	Emotional	Performance
Prompt 87	Self-assessment	Growth	Fulfillment	Optimization
Prompt 88	Self-assessment	Organizational	Reflection	Improvement
Prompt 89	Self-assessment	Executive	Priority	Organizational
Prompt 90	Skills	Introspection	Evolution	Self-Assessment
Prompt 91	Skills	Collaboration	Analytical	Innovation
Prompt 92	Strategies	Strategy	Efficiency	Planning
Prompt 93	Strength	Innate	Strengths-based	Introspection
Prompt 94	Strength	Innate	Gifts	Psychometric
Prompt 95	Strength	Self-awareness	Cohesion	Strengths-Utilization
Prompt 96	Strength	Alignment	Strengths	KPIs
Prompt 97	Strength	Indicators	Overutilization	Burnout
Prompt 98	Strength	Misrepresentation	Integrity	Realignment
Prompt 99	Strength	Development	Mastery	Productivity
Prompt 100	Support	Self-Confidence	Interventions	Metrics
Prompt 101	Support	Habits	Workflow	Stakeholder Buy-in
Prompt 102	Support	Resources	Communication	Opportunity
Prompt 103	Values	Priorities	Alignment	Team-Dynamics
Prompt 104	Values	Values	Relationships	Stakeholders
Prompt 105	Values	Behavior	Feedback	Nuanced
Prompt 106	Values	Integration	Reflective	Self-awareness
Prompt 107	Values	Openness	Fulfillment	HighPerformance
Prompt 108	Weakness	GoalAchievement	Weaknesses	PersonalGrowth
Prompt 109	Weakness	Weaknesses	Conversation	Risk-Assessment
Prompt 110	Weakness	Assessment	Career	Recognition
Prompt 111	Weakness	Transformation	Confidence	Communication

Appendix No 9

Unlock the Full Potential of This Book - Instantly

Dive into a world of convenience with our electronic copy! Feel free to seamlessly copy and paste any prompt that sparks your interest.

Customize them to fit your unique needs. Say goodbye to the hassle of retyping. Start crafting your perfect prompts with ease and efficiency!.

To access the electronic copy, please scan this QR code:

www.ingramcontent.com/pod-product-compliance
Lightning Source LLC
LaVergne TN
LVHW082036050326
832904LV00005B/200